See the Wider picture

The curious Cube Houses, Rotterdam, the Netherlands

These strange houses were designed in the 1970s. They are made in cube shapes turned on their points. This gives space for people to walk underneath. From a distance they look like a forest and the people who live in them feel like they are living in a tree village.

Would you like to live in a house like this?

CONTENTS

Starter unit — My world

0.1 2
0.2 3
0.3 4
0.4 5

Unit 1 — People are people

1.1 Vocabulary 6
1.2 Grammar 8
1.3 Reading and Vocabulary 9
1.4 Grammar 10
1.5 Listening and Vocabulary 11
1.6 Speaking 12
1.7 Writing 13
1.8 Self-assessment 14
1.9 Self-check 15
BBC Culture 16

Unit 2 — It's delicious!

2.1 Vocabulary 18
2.2 Grammar 20
2.3 Reading and Vocabulary 21
2.4 Grammar 22
2.5 Listening and Vocabulary 23
2.6 Speaking 24
2.7 English in use 25
2.8 Self-assessment 26
2.9 Self-check 27
BBC Culture 28

Unit 3 — Every day

3.1 Vocabulary 30
3.2 Grammar 32
3.3 Reading and Vocabulary 33
3.4 Grammar 34
3.5 Listening and Vocabulary 35
3.6 Speaking 36
3.7 Writing 37
3.8 Self-assessment 38
3.9 Self-check 39
BBC Culture 40

Unit 4 — Love to learn

4.1 Vocabulary 42
4.2 Grammar 44
4.3 Reading and Vocabulary 45
4.4 Grammar 46
4.5 Listening and Vocabulary 47
4.6 Speaking 48
4.7 English in use 49
4.8 Self-assessment 50
4.9 Self-check 51
BBC Culture 52

Unit 5 — The music of life

5.1 Vocabulary 54
5.2 Grammar 56
5.3 Reading and Vocabulary 57
5.4 Grammar 58
5.5 Listening and Vocabulary 59

Unit 5 (continued) — The music of life

5.6 Speaking 60
5.7 Writing 61
5.8 Self-assessment 62
5.9 Self-check 63
BBC Culture 64

Unit 6 — A question of sport

6.1 Vocabulary 66
6.2 Grammar 68
6.3 Reading and Vocabulary 69
6.4 Grammar 70
6.5 Listening and Vocabulary 71
6.6 Speaking 72
6.7 English in use 73
6.8 Self-assessment 74
6.9 Self-check 75
BBC Culture 76

Unit 7 — The time machine

7.1 Vocabulary 78
7.2 Grammar 80
7.3 Reading and Vocabulary 81
7.4 Grammar 82
7.5 Listening and Vocabulary 83
7.6 Speaking 84
7.7 Writing 85
7.8 Self-assessment 86
7.9 Self-check 87
BBC Culture 88

Unit 8 — Talking to the world

8.1 Vocabulary 90
8.2 Grammar 92
8.3 Reading and Vocabulary 93
8.4 Grammar 94
8.5 Listening and Vocabulary 95
8.6 Speaking 96
8.7 English in use 97
8.8 Self-assessment 98
8.9 Self-check 99
BBC Culture 100

Unit 9 — Getting around

9.1 Vocabulary 102
9.2 Grammar 104
9.3 Reading and Vocabulary 105
9.4 Grammar 106
9.5 Listening and Vocabulary 107
9.6 Speaking 108
9.7 Writing 109
9.8 Self-assessment 110
9.9 Self-check 111
BBC Culture 112

Exam time 1 114
Exam time 2 118
Exam time 3 122
Self-checks answer key 126

0

0.1 Subject pronouns; *to be;* possessive adjectives; spelling

My world

VOCABULARY
Possessions | Colours | Classroom language | Cardinal and ordinal numbers | Days of the week | Months | Seasons | Dates | Telling the time | Spelling?

GRAMMAR
Subject pronouns | *to be* | Possessive adjectives | Plural nouns | Demonstrative pronouns | Imperatives | Object pronouns | *wh-* questions

1 Match pictures A–F with subject pronouns 1–6.

A B C D E F

1 ☐ you
2 ☐ they
3 ☐ we
4 ☐ he
5 *A* I
6 ☐ she

2 Choose the correct option.

1 He *are* / *is* a teacher.
2 They *am* / *are* good friends.
3 She *is* / *am* a doctor.
4 I *are* / *am* fifteen.
5 We *are* / *is* English students.
6 You *are* / *is* from Paris.

3 Make the sentences in Exercise 2 negative.

1 *He isn't a teacher.*
2 ______
3 ______
4 ______
5 ______
6 ______

4 Change the sentences in Exercise 2 into questions. Write short answers.

1 *Is he a teacher?* ✗ *No, he isn't.*
2 ______ ✓ ______
3 ______ ✗ ______
4 ______ ✓ ______
5 ______ ✓ ______
6 ______ ✗ ______

5 Complete the sentences with possessive pronouns.

1 Miss Jones is *my* (I) teacher. She's great.
2 Pedro isn't in ______ (we) class. He's fifteen.
3 Is Jacky ______ (you) friend?
4 Jo and Ann are sisters. Coco is ______ (they) dog.
5 My brother is ten. ______ (he) name is Ricky.

6 02 Listen and write down the names.

1 *Brian Banks* is my English friend.
2 My friend is from ______ .
3 Her first name is ______ .
4 My French friend is ______ .
5 My town is ______ .

1 Match photos A–L with words 1–12.

1 [D] bag
2 [ ] bike
3 [ ] computer
4 [ ] guitar
5 [ ] laptop
6 [ ] skateboard
7 [ ] teddy
8 [ ] book
9 [ ] TV
10 [ ] watch
11 [ ] wallet
12 [ ] key

2 Look at the pictures and write the plurals.

1 *books* 2 ______
3 ______ 4 ______
5 ______ 6 ______
7 ______ 8 ______

3 Complete the sentences with *this*, *these*, *that* or *those*.

1 ↓ *This* book is interesting.
2 → *That* book isn't interesting.
3 ↓ ______ laptops are old.
4 ↓ ______ T-shirt is big.
5 → ______ bag is new.
6 ↓ ______ watch is very small.
7 → ______ skateboard is cheap.
8 → ______ TVs are good.

4 Order the letters and write the colours in the sentences.

1 The bus is *red* (der).
2 This is my ______ (lebu) dress.
3 The wallet is ______ (worbn).
4 His car is ______ (clakb).
5 The skateboard is ______ (greoan).
6 Katy's bag is ______ (lewoly).
7 Is his T-shirt ______ (neger)?

Imperatives; classroom language; object pronouns

1 **Order the words to make sentences.**

1 in / books / your / write / exercise
Write in your exercise books.
2 in / books / your / put / bags / your
______
3 page / to / fifteen / turn
______
4 five / at / exercise / look
______
5 books / your / open
______
6 partner / question / a / your / ask
______

2 **Look at the pictures and make negative imperatives. Use the phrases below.**

ask a question open your books sit down stand up ~~talk to your partner~~ write the answers

1

2

3

4

5

6

1 *Don't talk to your partner.*
2 ______
3 ______
4 ______
5 ______
6 ______

3 **Match 1–4 with a–d to make questions.**

1 [*d*] [*ii*] What's the English word
2 [ ] [ ] Which page
3 [ ] [ ] What's the spelling
4 [ ] [ ] What's

a are we on?
b the homework?
c of *coursebook*?
d for 'taxi'?

4 **Match the questions in Exercise 3 with these answers (i–iv).**

i C-O-U-R-S-E-B-O-O-K.
ii It's the same: 'taxi'!
iii Exercises 1 and 2 on page 22.
iv Page 175.

5 **Complete the sentences with object pronouns.**

1 Danny and Sue are happy. Look at *them* (they)!
2 This is her phone number. Phone ______ (she).
3 These are your books. Put ______ (they) on the desk.
4 My English is good. Ask ______ (I) a question!
5 Tom's answers are correct. Listen to ______ (he).
6 We're at home. Visit ______ (we) soon.

0.4 Cardinal and ordinal numbers; days of the week; months; seasons; dates; saying phone numbers; telling the time; *wh-* questions

1 Write the numbers in words.

1 600 *six hundred*
2 7,584 ______
3 259 ______
4 354 ______
5 22nd ______
6 53rd ______
7 11th ______
8 99th ______

2 Find the days, months and seasons below in the word search. Look ↑, ↓, ↗ and ↘.

Monday	March	spring
Tuesday	April	summer
Wednesday	July	
Friday	August	
Sunday	November	

S	Q	Q	I	A	S	L	F	T	T	S	E
T	I	O	J	U	L	Y	R	U	C	U	P
Z	S	E	S	G	A	G	I	E	N	M	Y
Q	N	M	I	U	N	I	D	S	U	M	S
B	A	O	U	S	N	A	A	D	N	E	O
R	N	N	V	T	S	D	Y	A	X	R	P
W	E	D	N	E	S	D	A	Y	I	C	I
L	A	A	V	A	M	H	P	Y	J	P	P
I	I	Y	D	P	C	B	A	S	F	T	K
L	S	R	C	R	T	L	E	R	R	S	G
R	K	N	A	I	F	D	A	R	H	C	Q
R	L	M	B	L	Q	S	P	R	I	N	G

3 03 Listen and write the dates.

1 *1st November*
2 ______
3 ______
4 ______
5 ______
6 ______

4 04 Listen and write the phone numbers.

1 *07825541923*
2 ______
3 ______
4 ______
5 ______
6 ______

5 Match pictures A–H with times 1–8.

A B C D E F G H

1 [E] nine o'clock
2 [ ] ten to nine
3 [ ] half past six
4 [ ] five past two
5 [ ] quarter past three
6 [ ] quarter to eight
7 [ ] twenty to one
8 [ ] eleven o'clock

6 Complete the questions with *who*, *what*, *where*, *when* or *how*.

1 *Who* are your teachers?
2 ______ is your surname?
3 ______ old is he?
4 ______ time is the lesson?
5 ______ are you from?
6 ______ is his birthday?
7 ______ is your favourite music?

7 Match questions 1–7 in Exercise 6 with answers a–g.

a [1] Mr Hands and Mrs Turner.
b [ ] Pop.
c [ ] Seventeen.
d [ ] Smith.
e [ ] London.
f [ ] 9.30.
g [ ] 4th November.

1

People are people

VOCABULARY
Nationalities | Family | Adjectives to describe people

GRAMMAR
can for ability | *have got*

READING
General appearance and personality

LISTENING
Clothes

SPEAKING
Greeting people and introducing others

WRITING
A short description of a person

BBC CULTURE
Can you remember thirty numbers?

1.1 VOCABULARY Nationalities; family; adjectives to describe people

I can talk about my family and nationalities.

1 Complete the names of the countries.

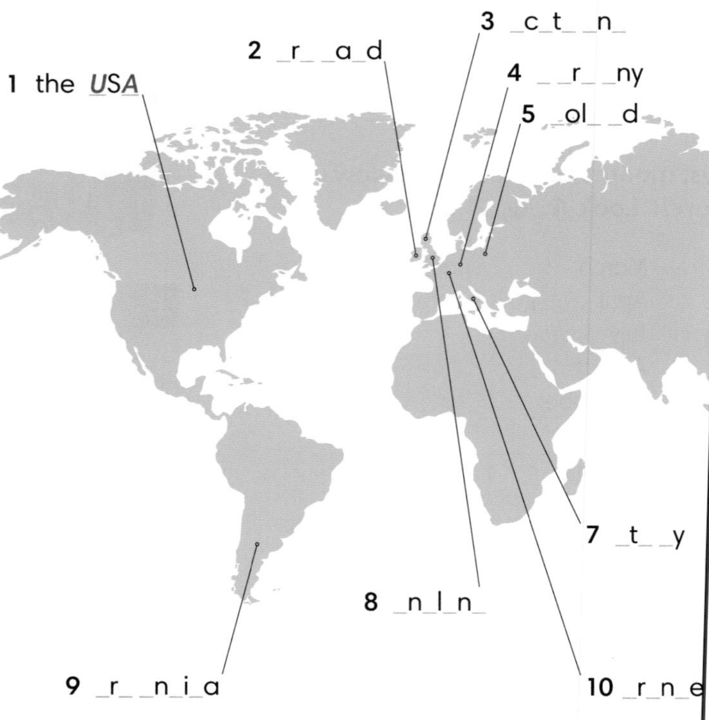

2 Write the nationalities for the countries in Exercise 1.

1 *American* 6 ______
2 ______ 7 ______
3 ______ 8 ______
4 ______ 9 ______
5 ______ 10 ______

3 Find eight family members in the word search. Look ↑, ↓, ↗ and ↘.

Z	N	R	T	E	A	M	H	T	I	E	R
O	Z	N	S	N	S	U	N	I	U	R	E
E	V	A	L	G	O	F	O	G	D	A	C
R	F	D	E	U	N	C	L	E	A	D	T
K	L	N	A	V	S	E	O	T	U	L	R
B	I	S	S	B	U	E	N	S	G	T	R
H	S	C	U	H	R	U	Y	R	H	E	H
Z	W	I	F	E	A	O	B	O	T	S	A
S	S	K	A	L	J	I	T	S	E	K	K
N	N	L	A	P	K	M	I	H	R	U	L
F	M	Q	C	O	U	S	I	N	E	J	S
S	T	F	Q	L	T	N	Z	D	H	R	O

4 ●● Look at the diagram and complete the sentences with the correct words.

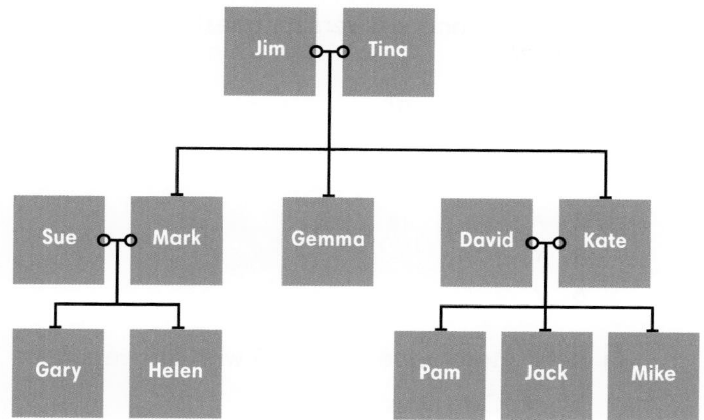

1 Jack is Mike's *brother* .
2 Tina is Pam's ______ .
3 Helen is ______ sister.
4 David is ______ husband.
5 Gemma is Mike's ______ .
6 Gary is Jack's ______ .
7 Jim is Gary's ______ .
8 Gemma is Tina's ______ .

5 ● Read the sentences. Add 's or an apostrophe (').

1 My cousin's friend is English.
2 Jack dad car is Japanese.
3 James dog is black.
4 Ella mum is Rita.
5 My brothers names are Pete and Mark.

6 ● WORD FRIENDS Choose the correct option.

1 Dan's hair is *young* / *long.*
2 The girl's hair is *blonde* / *big.*
3 Tom's eyes are *blue* / *tall.*
4 My sister is *slim* / *green.*
5 The teacher is *long* / *short.*

7 ● Find and correct the mistakes in the sentences.

1 Jack is my friend brother.
Jack is my friend's brother.
2 Hans is Germany.
______
3 My granny is young. She's ninety-four.
______
4 Lukes car is from the USA.
______
5 Your hair is small.
______
6 My sister husband is Charlie.
______
7 Eva is from Argentinian.
______

8 ●● Complete the word puzzle. What's the hidden word?

1 *d a u g h t e r*
2
3
4
5
6
7
8
9

1 Gary is Sonia's dad. Sonia is Gary's ______ .
2 I'm from France. I'm ______ .
3 My granddad's hair isn't long and dark. It's short and ______ .
4 They're Irish. They're from ______ .
5 My hair isn't short. It's ______ .
6 My sister is Katy and my ______ is Dan.
7 My aunt is my uncle's ______ .
8 Yumiko is from Japan. She's ______ .
9 Helena isn't short. She's ______ .

The hidden word is: ______ .

9 ●●● Choose the correct option.

My [1]*friend's* / *friends* name is Eva. She's fifteen years [2]*young* / *old* and she's [3]*France* / *French*. She's [4]*from* / *of* Paris. Her brother's name [5]*is* / *are* Christophe and he's ten. Her [6]*daughter* / *sister*, Marie, is a baby. She's six months old. Eva is [7]*tall* / *long* and her hair is [8]*blonde* / *big*. She's a good friend.

1.2 GRAMMAR *can* for ability

I can use *can* to talk about abilities.

1 ● **Make sentences using *can*.**

1 Jack / speak / Japanese
Jack can speak Japanese.
2 I / swim / a kilometre
______
3 Keiko / write / a letter in English
______
4 Jim / drive / a car
______
5 Pat's brothers / fly / a plane
______
6 Gemma's baby / say / 'mama' and 'dada'
______

2 ● **Make the sentences in Exercise 1 negative.**

1 *Jack can't speak Japanese.*
2 ______
3 ______
4 ______
5 ______
6 ______

3 ● **Order the words to make questions.**

1 speak / you / German / can / ?
Can you speak German?
2 Mark / car / can / a / drive / ?
______
3 French / they / at / can / school / learn / ?
______
4 sister / Italian / your / understand / can / ?
______
5 Tina's / walk / baby / can / ?
______
6 play / can / brother / your / football / ?
______
7 kilometres / swim / many / you / how / can / ?
______

4 ● **Write short answers for questions 1–6 in Exercise 3.**

1 ✓ *Yes, I can.*
2 ✗ ______
3 ✗ ______
4 ✓ ______
5 ✗ ______
6 ✓ ______

5 ●● **Match questions 1–5 with answers a–e.**

1 [b] Can Daisy walk?
2 [ ] How many languages can you speak?
3 [ ] Can you stay under water?
4 [ ] Can Dan sing?
5 [ ] Can Jack and Natasha drive?

a Yes, I can – two minutes.
b No, she can't. She's six months old.
c No, he can't.
d Yes, they can. They've got a nice car.
e Two – Polish and Spanish.

6 ●●● **Complete the dialogue with *can* or *can't*.**

A: That's a nice photo. Who is it?
B: It's my brother. He's in France now. He's at an international school.
A: Oh. [1]*Can* he speak French?
B: Yes, he [2]______ . He [3]______ speak French and he [4]______ read French. He [5]______ also play tennis. It's an international tennis school!
A: That's good. I [6]______ speak French and I [7]______ play tennis. Maybe he [8]______ teach me!

I can find specific detail in an article and talk about general appearance and personality.

1 Read the text. Match photos A–C with paragraphs 2–4.

The Hemsworths

1 Chris and Liam Hemsworth are brothers. They're from Australia. Their grandfather is Dutch, from the Netherlands, and there is also English, Irish, Scottish and German in their family – it's very international! Chris and Liam are young, tall and handsome. They are also famous. They are very good actors.

2 In family photographs their hair is short, their eyes are blue and they aren't very different. But in the films that isn't true! They are completely different.

3 Liam is twenty-seven and he's Gale in the three *Hunger Games* films. He's Katniss's friend. He can fight and hunt and he can shoot arrows, like Katniss. In the film his hair is short and dark. He's very brave and strong. He's also an angry young man.

4 Chris is thirty-two and he is Thor, the superhero, in the *Thor* and *Avengers* films. He's big and strong. His hair is long and blonde. He can shoot lightning. Gale can't do that!

A ☐

B ☐

C ☐

2 Read the text again. Match headings a–d with paragraphs 1–4.

a ☐ Not a man, a god
b ☐ A good friend and a brave hunter
c ☐ Similar or different?
d ☐ Acting brothers

3 Read the text again. Mark the sentences ✓ (right), ✗ (wrong) or ? (doesn't say).

1 ☐ Chris and Liam are from Scotland.
2 ☐ Their father is an actor.
3 ☐ Chris and Liam's hair is long and blonde.
4 ☐ Chris and Liam are in different films.
5 ☐ They are the same age.
6 ☐ Gale and Thor can do the same things.

4 Choose the correct option.

1 Tommy is *(clever)* / *brave*. He's a university teacher.
2 Gemma is *friendly* / *nervous*. Her exams are soon.
3 Terry is *funny* / *quiet*. He's always in his room.
4 Tim can fight anybody. He's strong and *nice* / *brave*.

1.4 GRAMMAR *have got*

I can use *have got* to talk about possessions.

1 ● Complete the sentences with *have got* or *has got*.

1 Pete *has got* a dictionary.
2 I ______ a blog.
3 Jim and Dave ______ a dog.
4 We ______ a wonderful teacher.
5 My mum ______ two sisters.
6 Our dad ______ a red car.
7 Jack ______ a big family.

2 ● Make the sentences negative.

1 I've got red hair.
I haven't got red hair.
2 We've got a small house.
______
3 My cousin's got a selfie stick.
______
4 The students have got homework today.
______
5 Katy's dad has got a job.
______
6 Ella's got a baby brother.
______
7 I've got a laptop.
______

3 ● Make questions using *have got*.

1 Eddie / a German friend / ?
Has Eddie got a German friend?
2 we / an Art lesson today / ?
______
3 Paul and Helen / a big house / ?
______
4 your brother / an interesting job / ?
______
5 you / a good dictionary / ?
______
6 your teacher / children / ?
______
7 your laptop / a camera / ?
______

4 ● Write short answers for the questions in Exercise 3.

1 ✓ *Yes, he has.*
2 ✗ ______
3 ✓ ______
4 ✓ ______
5 ✗ ______
6 ✓ ______
7 ✗ ______

5 ●● Complete the dialogues with one or two words in each gap.

1 A: *Have* you got a brother?
B: ______, I have. His name's Tom.
2 A: Have we ______ French today?
B: No, we ______. We've got French on Friday.
3 A: ______ our teacher got a car?
B: No. She ______ got a car. She's got a bicycle.
4: A: How ______ sisters has Dave got?
B: ______ got one sister.
5 A: ______ you got your camera and selfie stick?
B: ______ got my camera but I ______ got my selfie stick. It's at home.
6 A: ______ Thor got dark hair?
B: ______, he hasn't. He's got blonde hair.

6 ●●● Complete the email with the words below.

can't ~~from~~ got hasn't have he's I've you

To: hello@ricky.com

Hi Ricky,

My name's Bess and I'm [1]*from* London. I've got a big family. [2]______ got three sisters and one brother. My brother's twenty and [3]______ got a car. My sisters [4]______ got blonde hair but my brother [5]______. He's got short dark hair. My mum's [6]______ a job in my school. She's a teacher. I've got a lot of hobbies – art, films, music and books. But I [7]______ do sports.

And you? Have [8]______ got a big family? Have you got a cat or dog? I haven't. What are your hobbies?

Write soon,

Bess

1.5 LISTENING and VOCABULARY You've got style!

I can identify specific information in a conversation and talk about clothes.

1 Match words 1–11 with A–K in the pictures.

1 [G] jeans
2 [ ] shoes
3 [ ] hat
4 [ ] sunglasses
5 [ ] sweatshirt
6 [ ] dress
7 [ ] boots
8 [ ] shorts
9 [ ] trainers
10 [ ] T-shirt
11 [ ] jacket

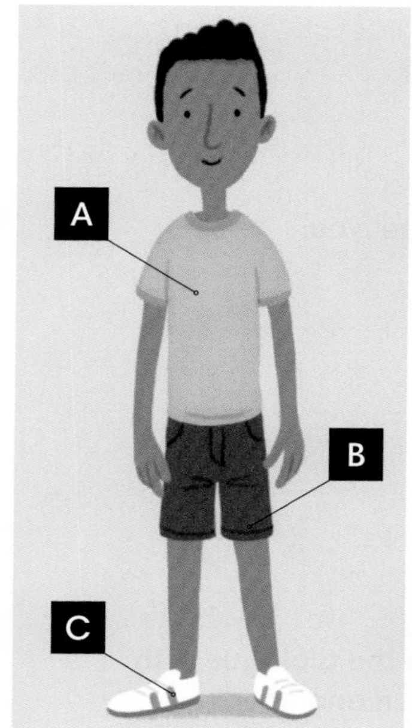

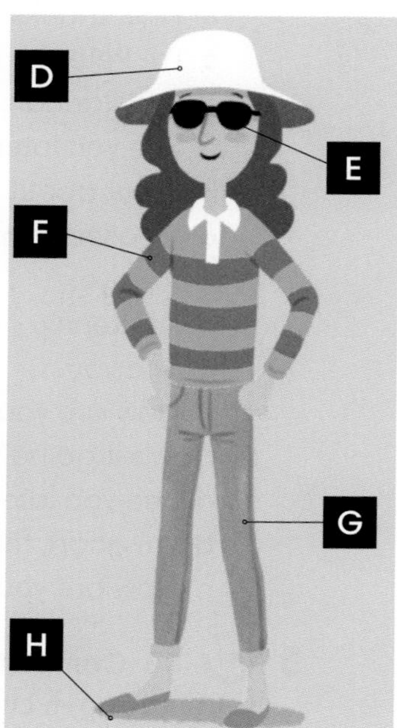

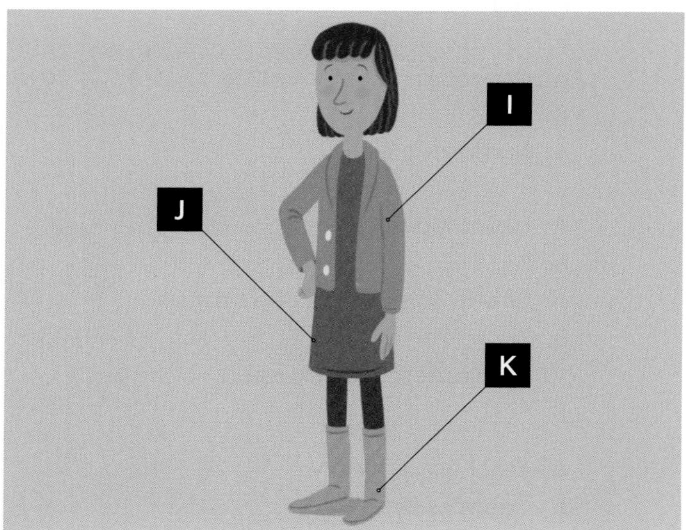

2 Order the letters and write the words in the sentences.

1 I've got a new *tracksuit* (sturcakit) for football practice.
2 It's very cold. Where are my __________ (storreus)?
3 My dad's got a nice white __________ (thisr) for his job.
4 Terry's new __________ (stobo) are brown.
5 My __________ (tweeras) is from Paris.
6 Jacky's __________ (trisk) is black and white and quite short.

3 Complete the compliments with the words below.

nice really ~~style~~ thanks your

1 You've got great *style* .
2 Your hat is __________ cool.
3 I like __________ T-shirt.
4 A: Your hair is fantastic!
B: __________ !
5 The colour is very __________ .

4 05 Listen and match the names (1–3) with the screens (A–C).

Have You got Style?

A B C

1 [ ] Jo 2 [ ] Lee 3 [ ] Tara

5 05 Listen again. Mark the sentences T (true) or F (false).

1 [ ] Tara is fifteen.
2 [ ] She's got a cat on her T-shirt.
3 [ ] Her hair is always the same colour.
4 [ ] Jo is thirty-five.
5 [ ] Her clothes are always black.
6 [ ] Her clothes are from a market.
7 [ ] Lee is from London.
8 [ ] She's got lots of boots.

1.6 SPEAKING Meeting people

I can greet people and introduce others.

1 Match 1–5 with a–e to make phrases.

OUT of class

1 [e] Come — a about her?
2 [ ] No — b me.
3 [ ] What — c cool!
4 [ ] Excuse — d worries!
5 [ ] Really — e on!

2 Complete the dialogues with phrases from Exercise 1.

OUT of class

1 A: We're late! *Come on!*
B: OK, I'm ready!
2 A: Look – the girl with blonde hair.
B: ______
A: She's a famous singer!
3 A: ______ Are you Tom's sister?
B: No, I'm not. I'm his cousin.
4 A: Look! It's Katy Perry!
B: Wow! This is ______ !
5 A: Oh – you're not Katy Perry. I'm sorry!
B: ______

3 Order the words to make sentences.

1 you / are / how / ?
How are you?
2 it / going / how's / ?
______
3 fine / I'm
______
4 thanks / good, / I'm
______
5 Kim / name's / my
______
6 Lee / I'm
______
7 meet / to / pleased / you
______
8 my / is / friend, / this / Di
______
9 later / you / see
______
10 to / nice / you, / meet / Emma
______

4 Choose the correct response.

1 Hello!
(a) Hi!
b Good, thanks.
c See you.
2 How are you?
a How's it going?
b Fine, thanks.
c I'm Pete.
3 This is Hannah.
a See you later.
b What about her?
c Pleased to meet you.
4 Goodbye.
a I'm Kenny.
b See you.
c How are you?
5 How's it going?
a See you later.
b I'm good, thanks.
c How are you?

5 06 Complete the dialogue with sentences a–f. Listen and check.

A: Hello.
B: 1 *d*
A: Are you a new student?
B: 2 ______
A: My name's Bill.
B: 3 ______
A: How's it going?
B: 4 ______
A: Great! This is Beth. She's my sister.
B: 5 ______
A: No worries. See you later.
B: 6 ______

a Yes, I am. I'm Amy.
b See you. Bye!
c Hi, Beth. I'm sorry. I'm late for my English class.
d Hi!
e Good, thanks. The teachers are nice here. It's really cool!
f Nice to meet you, Bill!

I can write a short description of a person.

1 **Complete the description with the words below.**

but ~~cousin~~ different famous friendly long sixteen speak style

My famous friend

Annie Parker is my [1]*cousin*. She's also my best friend. Annie is [2]________ years old and she's great. She's pretty. She's got [3]________, blonde hair and blue eyes. Annie's got great [4]________! She's always got lovely clothes.

Annie is funny and [5]________, and she's clever too. She can [6]________ four languages. She's also brave. Annie can't walk [7]________ she isn't sad. She's got a special electric chair so she can move. She can sing. In our town Annie is [8]________. She's often on the radio! Now she's a student but her dream job is to be a singer, like Taylor Swift. Perhaps she can sing in [9]________ languages and everyone in the world can know about her! Yes, she can do it!

2 **Read the description again. Answer the questions.**

1 What has Annie got?

____

2 What can Annie do?

____

3 What can't Annie do?

____

3 **Match sentences 1–6 with the parts of the description a–f.**

1 [*f*] Her dream job is to be a singer.
2 [ ] Annie Parker is my cousin.
3 [ ] She's also very brave.
4 [ ] Annie's got great style.
5 [ ] Yes, she can do it.
6 [ ] Annie is sixteen years old.

a appearance
b personality
c ending
d age
e introduction
f plan

4 **Join the sentences with *and* or *but*.**

1 He's got a brother. He's got a sister.
He's got a brother and a sister.
2 Annie can't walk. She isn't sad.
____
3 Tim can sing. He can't dance.
____
4 She can speak French. She can't speak German.
____
5 She's clever. She's funny.
____
6 She can play the guitar. She can play the piano.
____

5 **Write notes about a friend.**

Age: ________
Nationality: ________
Languages: ________
Family: ________
Appearance: ________
Personality: ________
Positive things about the person:
____
Why this person is important to you:
____

6 **Write a description of your friend. Remember to do these things.**

- Use your notes from Exercise 5.
- Join some sentences with *and* or *but*.
- Start with a simple introduction and finish with a simple ending.
- Write 70–100 words.

1.8 SELF-ASSESSMENT

For each learning objective, tick (✓) the box that best matches your ability.

☺☺ = I understand and can help a friend.

☺ = I understand and can do it by myself.

☹ = I understand but have some questions.

☹☹ = I do not understand.

		☺☺	☺	☹	☹☹	Need help?	Now try ...
1.1	Vocabulary					Students' Book pp. 10–11 Workbook pp. 6–7	Ex. 1–3, p. 15
1.2	Grammar					Students' Book p. 12 Workbook p. 8	Ex. 4, p. 15
1.3	Reading					Students' Book p. 13 Workbook p. 9	
1.4	Grammar					Students' Book p. 14 Workbook p. 10	Ex. 5, p. 15
1.5	Listening					Students' Book p. 15 Workbook p. 11	
1.6	Speaking					Students' Book p. 16 Workbook p. 12	Ex. 6–7, p. 15
1.7	Writing					Students' Book p. 17 Workbook p. 13	

1.1 I can talk about my family and nationalities.
1.2 I can use *can* to talk about abilities.
1.3 I can find specific detail in an article and talk about general appearance and personality.
1.4 I can use *have got* to talk about possession.
1.5 I can identify specific detail in a conversation and talk about clothes.
1.6 I can greet people and introduce others.
1.7 I can write a short description of a person.

What can you remember from this unit?

New words I learned (the words you most want to remember from this unit)	**Expressions and phrases I liked** (any expressions or phrases you think sound nice, useful or funny)	**English I heard or read outside class** (e.g. from websites, books, adverts, films, music)

1.9 SELF-CHECK

Vocabulary

1 Write the countries and nationalities.

1 My friend Pat is from Ireland. She's ________ .
2 My cousin Jake is from the USA. He's ________ .
3 My grandad is Italian. He's from ________ .
4 My aunt is from Poland. She's ________ .
5 Our teacher is French. She's from ________ .
6 My uncle is German. He's from ________ .

2 Write the family words.

1 My father's sister is my ________ .
2 My sister is my mother's ________ .
3 My mother is my father's ________ .
4 My father's mother is my ________ .
5 My brother is my mother's ________ .
6 My mother's husband is my ________ .

3 Choose the odd one out.

1	pink	red	green	slim
2	boots	shoes	hat	trainers
3	sunglasses	T-shirt	sweater	shirt
4	jeans	dress	trousers	shorts
5	small	tall	blonde	brave
6	friendly	grey	funny	clever

Grammar

4 Make sentences using *can*.

1 you / speak / German / ?
____
2 my sister / not / walk / ten kilometres
____
3 we / learn / Spanish / at my school
____
4 A: your brother / play / football / ?
B: yes / he
____
____
5 where / we / buy / new trainers / ?
____
6 our teacher / not / find / our homework
____
7 A: you / do / this excercise / ?
B: no / I
____
____
8 they / not / help / us
____

5 Write negative sentences and questions.

1 Gina's got a nice dress for the party.
✗ ________
? ________
2 You've got two brothers.
✗ ________
? ________
3 Pete and Tom have got a new car.
✗ ________
? ________
4 We've got an English test today.
✗ ________
? ________
5 I've got a problem with my computer.
✗ ________
? ________
6 Grant's got a black jacket.
✗ ________
? ________
7 Ian's sister's got long hair.
✗ ________
? ________

Speaking language practice

6 Match sentences 1–5 with responses a–e.

1 ☐ I love your hat.
2 ☐ I'm sorry I can't help.
3 ☐ She's got great style.
4 ☐ The party's at 7.30.
5 ☐ Excuse me. Are you Andy's brother?

a No worries.
b Yes! Nice to meet you.
c Yes. Her hair is fantastic.
d We're late. Come on!
e Thanks! Yours is really cool too!

7 Complete the dialogues with one or two words in each gap.

a A: Hi, Dan. How's it [1] ________ ?
B: I'm [2] ________ , thanks.

b A: Hi, Susie. [3] ________ are you?
B: [4] ________ good, thanks.
[5] ________ is my friend Robby.
A: Pleased to [6] ________ you, Robby.
My [7] ________ Jan.
B: [8] ________ to meet you, Jan.

c A: Look at the time! [9] ________
you later!
B: Bye!

1 Match pictures A–F with words 1–6.

A
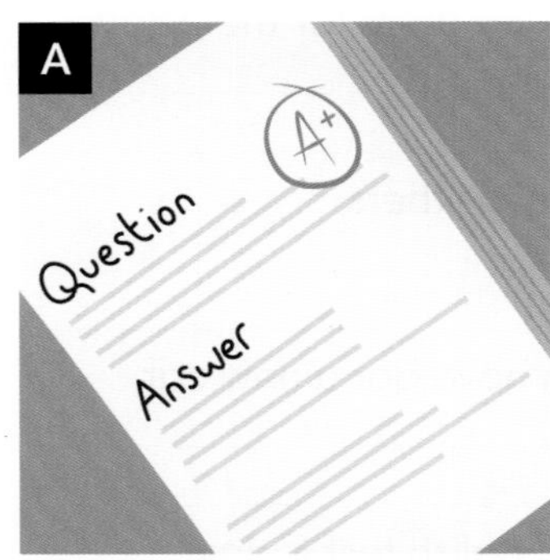

B
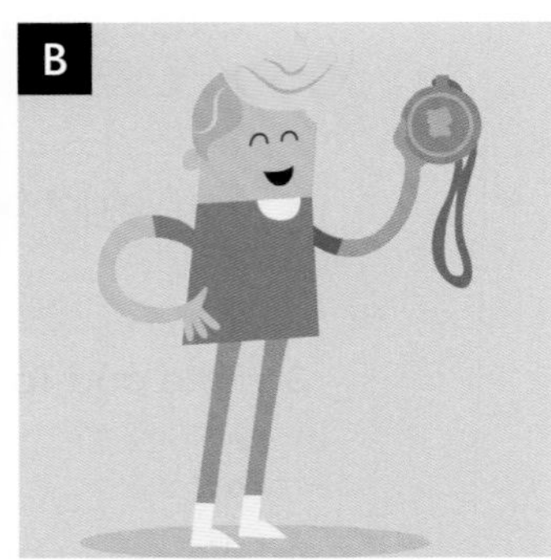

C

D

E
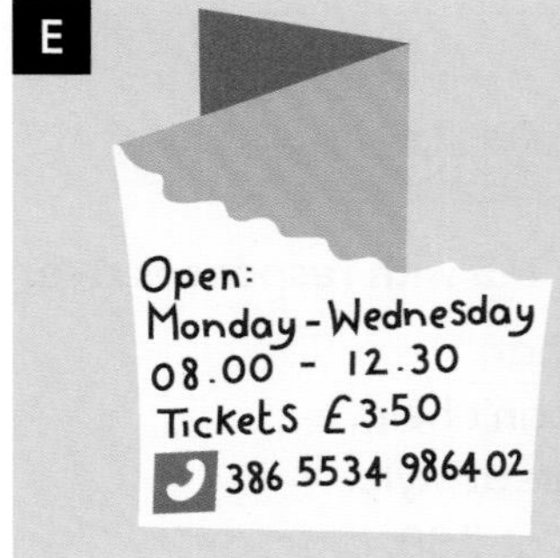

F

1 [C] zoo
2 [ ] lesson
3 [ ] list
4 [ ] information
5 [ ] winner
6 [ ] test

2 Complete the sentences with the words below.

champion competition fantastic
junior ~~memory~~

1 I've got a bad *memory* . I can't remember names or numbers!
2 Kim is ten. She's at ________ school.
3 I'm in a ________ on Saturday. I hope I win!
4 This book is very, very good. It's ________ !
5 My friend is a tennis ________ !

3 Complete the words.

1 This person can play a violin: v*iolinis*t
2 You can win this in a competition: pr_z_
3 This is a very clever child: pr_d_g_
4 You can see this from a car or a room: v_ _w
5 This person can write books: wr_t_r
6 You can be this before a test: n_rv_ _s
7 You can have a party on this day: b_rthd_ _

4 Find eight words from Exercises 1–3 in the word search. Look ↑, ↓, ↗ and ↘.

T	T	M	C	(L	I	S	T)
N	E	P	R	I	Z	E	T
E	S	W	I	N	N	E	R
M	T	G	M	E	Z	I	R
E	V	I	E	W	S	T	L
M	P	R	O	D	I	G	Y
O	E	O	M	O	R	Y	R
R	Z	S	O	J	D	Y	Y
Y	E	O	T	Z	G	C	E

5 Choose the correct option.

1 My brother's got (*prizes*) / *winners* in his room.
2 Have you got the shopping *test* / *list*?
3 I can't understand this *writer* / *information*. When is the shop open?
4 It's Tom's *birthday* / *test* on Monday. I've got a present for him. It's a new T-shirt.
5 I've got a *champion* / *competition* today. I'm *fantastic* / *nervous*!
6 She's a *prodigy* / *junior*. She's three years old and she can play the violin!

6 **Read the video script. Underline any words or phrases you don't know and find their meaning in your dictionary.**

Child prodigies

Part 1

These young people are here in London for an important competition. They're violin players. They're all very young and very good. They come from different countries – from the USA, from Japan, from Germany and many more. Samuel Tan is only eleven years old. He's from Singapore and he's got lots of prizes from competitions. Can he win this competition? Maybe he can. Juliette Russe is English – from London – and she's nervous. She thinks playing the violin is hard work. This competition is difficult. There are lots of great players. It's called The Yehudi Menuhin Competition. This year it's the famous violinist's one hundredth birthday! Good luck, everyone. Great music and a great view of London!

Part 2

This is Anushka with her family. They're very proud. Anushka's got the results of a difficult test. Now she's in a special club. It's called Mensa and it's a club for very, very clever people. Anushka is only eleven, but she got top marks. Anushka can do lots of things. She's got a wonderful memory. She can answer very hard questions. She can play the violin. But her favourite hobbies are reading and writing stories. She's got a blog and maybe one day she can be a writer. It's her dream job.

2

It's delicious!

VOCABULARY
Food and drink | Meals | Places to eat | Cooking | Popular supermarket foods

GRAMMAR
there is/there are + some/any | Countable and uncountable nouns | Quantifiers

READING
Preparing food

LISTENING
Shopping for food

SPEAKING
Ordering food

ENGLISH IN USE
too much/too many, not enough

BBC CULTURE
Can a robot cook?

2.1 VOCABULARY Food and drink

I can talk about food and drink.

1 Write the words below in the correct column.

~~apples~~ bacon burger butter carrots celery crisps grapes milk orange juice

Fruit	Vegetables	Meat	Drinks	Other
apples				

2 Match the words below with photos 1–9.

bananas ~~biscuits~~ chicken cola eggs milkshake muffin potatoes yoghurt

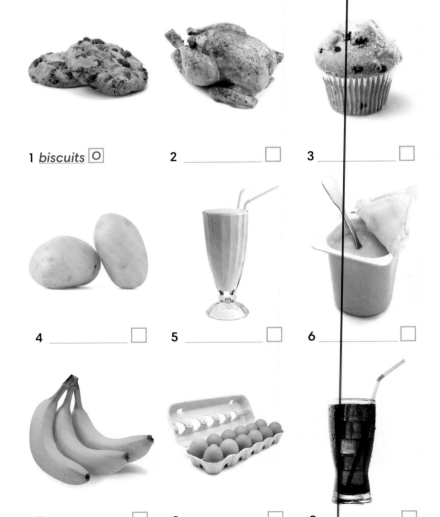

1 *biscuits* O

2 ______ ☐

3 ______ ☐

4 ______ ☐

5 ______ ☐

6 ______ ☐

7 ______ ☐

8 ______ ☐

9 ______ ☐

3 Mark the words in Exercise 2 F (fruit), V (vegetables), M (meat) or O (other).

4 ● Find eight words from Exercises 1–3 in the word search. Look ↑, ↓, ↗ and ↘.

V	E	L	A	L	L	E	C	N	T	S	G
R	R	R	O	H	C	D	D	R	R	E	B
X	I	D	E	R	T	B	U	T	T	E	R
D	S	C	E	G	(C	H	I	C	K	E	N)
R	J	S	P	S	G	U	T	C	S	X	I
G	E	E	B	O	R	S	S	E	L	A	C
R	T	Y	Y	F	T	B	P	M	R	V	C
M	I	L	K	S	H	A	R	Y	R	E	X
Z	R	T	E	A	R	C	T	L	A	G	R
F	D	E	K	G	Y	O	C	O	E	A	N
O	N	E	T	O	N	N	F	E	E	E	O
B	G	N	Q	I	E	V	F	H	L	S	U

5 ●● **Complete the sentences with words from Exercise 4.**

1 My sister's got a *chicken* in her garden. We have __________ for breakfast when we visit.
2 I can't make toast – there's no __________ .
3 Crisps are from __________ .
4 I always have __________ in my coffee.
5 People make wine from __________ .
6 Our dog can't eat __________ like apples or grapes; it's bad for him. Meat and vegetables are OK.
7 I love __________ with bits of fruit in it.

6 ● **Complete the words for meals 1–3. Match them with photos A–C.**

1 ☐ In the morning: **b**_ _ _ _ _ _ _ _
2 ☐ In the middle of the day: **l**_ _ _ _
3 ☐ In the evening: **d**_ _ _ _ _

A

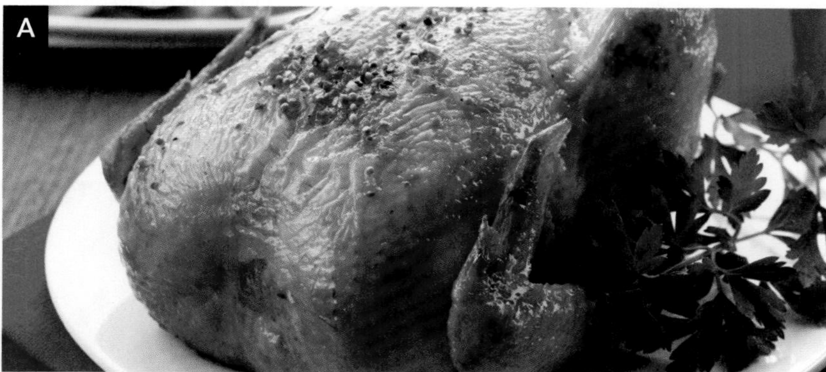

B

C

7 ●● **Order the letters and write the words in the sentences.**

1 Our *lunch* (nuclh) is usually at 12.30.
2 I've got a cheese __________ (swidchan) but I haven't got an __________ (leppa).
3 There's __________ (klim) and __________ (olac) in the fridge.
4 What's your favourite __________ (fetrabsak)?
5 My brother can cook. Tonight we've got __________ (heknicc) for __________ (rindne).
6 __________ (sifnumf) are delicious but they aren't good for you!
7 Let's have something to drink. An orange __________ (ejiuc) for me and a chocolate __________ (msilkhkae) for you!
8 Vegetables like __________ (rcrtaso) and __________ (crleey) are very good for you.

8 ●●● **Complete the words in the dialogue.**

A: What's your favourite [1]m*eal*?
B: That's [2]b_ _ _ _ _ _ _ _: [3]e_ _ _ and [4]b_ _ _ _, toast and [5]c_ _ _ l.
A: That's hundreds of [6]c_ _ _ _ _ _ s!
B: Yes, but it's [7]d_ l_ _ _ _ _ _! And [8]l_ _ _ _ at school is only an [9]a_ _ _ _ and a [10]c_ _ _ _ _ sandwich. What about you?
A: Oh, easy – [11]d_ _ _ _ _! [12]C_ _ _ k_ _ or fish, lots of [13]v_ _ _ _ _ _ _ _ _, [14]y_ _ _ _ _ _ and water. It's all good for me.
B: No muffins or [15]b_ _ _ u_ _ _?
A: Never!
B: That's boring.
A: No, it's good!

2.2 GRAMMAR *there is/there are*

I can use *there is/there are* to talk about places to eat in town.

1 Complete the words for places to eat.

1 burger bar
2 c_f_
3 f_st f_ _d r_st_ _r_nt
4 s_ndw_ch b_r
5 v_g_t_r_ _n c_f_
6 r_st_ _r_nt
7 p_zz_r_ _

2 Complete the sentences with *is* or *are*.

1 There *is* an expensive restaurant.
2 There _____ some cheap cafés.
3 There _____ a nice pizzeria.
4 There _____ some fast food restaurants.
5 There _____ some Chinese restaurants.
6 There _____ a big burger bar.
7 There _____ a vegeterian restaurant.
8 There _____ some French restaurants.

3 Make the sentences in Exercise 2 negative.

1 *There isn't an expensive restaurant.*
2 ______
3 ______
4 ______
5 ______
6 ______
7 ______
8 ______

4 Write questions and short answers for the sentences in Exercise 3.

1 ? *Is there an expensive restaurant?*
✗ *No, there isn't.*
2 ? ______
✓ ______
3 ? ______
✓ ______
4 ? ______
✓ ______
5 ? ______
✗ ______
6 ? ______
✗ ______
7 ? ______
✓ ______
8 ? ______
✗ ______

5 Make sentences.

1 there / not / apples / on the table
There aren't any apples on the table.
2 there / not / biscuits / in the box
______
3 there / a vegetarian café / in the town centre / ?
______
4 there / a pizza / in the fridge / ?
______
5 there / not / a burger bar / near our school
______
6 there / not / potatoes / in the kitchen
______
7 there / not / Italian restaurants in my town
______
8 there / eggs / in the fridge / ?
______

6 Complete the dialogue with the words below.

any are is isn't it's some there ~~there's~~

A: [1]*There's* a new restaurant in our town.
B: Really? [2]_____ it a Chinese restaurant? Chinese meals are my favourite.
A: No, it [3]_____ . It's French. It's very nice and the menu's great.
B: Are there [4]_____ vegetarian meals?
A: Yes, there [5]_____ . They've got lots of salads. Oh and there are [6]_____ delicious cakes!
B: Are [7]_____ any pizzas on the menu?
A: No, there aren't! [8]_____ a French restaurant – it's not Italian!

2.3 READING and VOCABULARY What can you do with a potato?

I can find specific detail in a blog entry and talk about preparing food.

1 Look at the photos and complete the words.

1 bo*wl*

2 p_ _ _ _

3 f_ _ _

4 f_ _ _ _ _ p_ _

5 s_ _ _

6 p_ _ _ _ _

2 WORD FRIENDS Complete the sentences with the verbs below.

add bake ~~beat~~ boil cut fry

1 *Beat* two eggs in a bowl.
2 ________ some salt and pepper.
3 ________ the cake for twenty minutes.
4 ________ the water and then add the pasta.
5 ________ up the onion and ________ it in the oil.

3 Read the blog. Look at the pictures below and write the verbs.

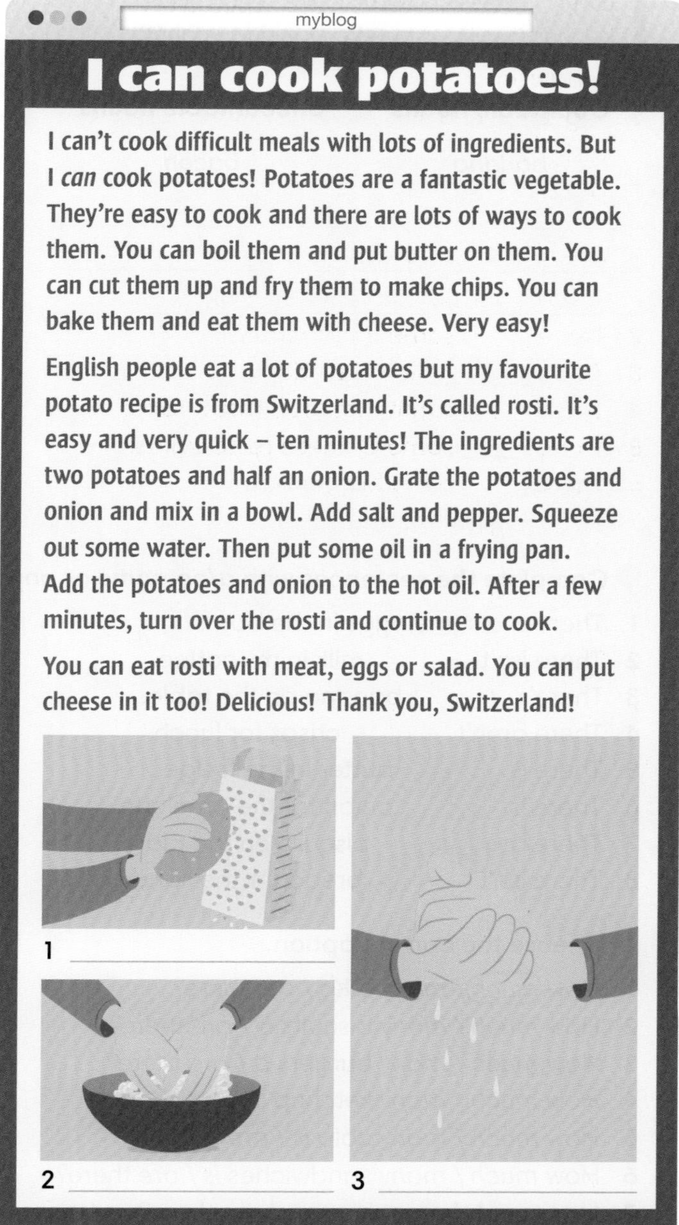

myblog

I can cook potatoes!

I can't cook difficult meals with lots of ingredients. But I *can* cook potatoes! Potatoes are a fantastic vegetable. They're easy to cook and there are lots of ways to cook them. You can boil them and put butter on them. You can cut them up and fry them to make chips. You can bake them and eat them with cheese. Very easy!

English people eat a lot of potatoes but my favourite potato recipe is from Switzerland. It's called rosti. It's easy and very quick – ten minutes! The ingredients are two potatoes and half an onion. Grate the potatoes and onion and mix in a bowl. Add salt and pepper. Squeeze out some water. Then put some oil in a frying pan. Add the potatoes and onion to the hot oil. After a few minutes, turn over the rosti and continue to cook.

You can eat rosti with meat, eggs or salad. You can put cheese in it too! Delicious! Thank you, Switzerland!

1 ________
2 ________
3 ________

4 Read the blog again. Answer the questions.

1 How many ideas for cooking potatoes are there in the text?
____
2 Where is rosti from?
____
3 What are the ingredients for rosti?
____
4 How long is it to cook rosti?
____
5 How many things can you eat with rosti?
____

2.4 GRAMMAR Countable and uncountable nouns; quantifiers

I can use countable and uncountable nouns and talk about quantities of food.

1 Write the words below in the correct column.

~~bacon~~ ~~banana~~ biscuit bread burger carrot cheese cola crisp egg juice ketchup milk omelette onion yoghurt

Countable nouns	Uncountable nouns
banana	*bacon*

2 Complete the sentences with *a/an*, *some* or *any*.

1 There are *some* eggs in the bowl.
2 There isn't ______ milk in my coffee.
3 There's ______ banana on the table.
4 There aren't ______ crisps for lunch.
5 There is ______ butter in the fridge.
6 There is ______ onion for the omelette.
7 There are ______ biscuits on the plate.
8 There isn't ______ bread for the sandwiches.

3 Choose the correct option.

1 How (much) / *many* oil (is) / *are* there?
2 How *much* / *many* biscuits *is* / *are* there?
3 How *much* / *many* burgers *is* / *are* there?
4 How *much* / *many* ketchup *is* / *are* there?
5 How *much* / *many* cola *is* / *are* there?
6 How *much* / *many* sandwiches *is* / *are* there?
7 How *much* / *many* eggs *is* / *are* there?
8 How *much* / *many* juice *is* / *are* there?

4 Choose the correct response.

1 How much milk is there?
 (a) There's a lot.
 b There isn't many.
 c There are lots.
2 How many biscuits are there?
 a There isn't much.
 b There aren't any.
 c There is a lot.
3 How much cheese is there?
 a There aren't many.
 b There isn't much.
 c There aren't any.
4 How much butter is there?
 a There isn't many.
 b There isn't any.
 c There are lots.
5 How many bananas are there?
 a There aren't much.
 b There isn't many.
 c There aren't many.

5 Complete the phrases with the words below. **OUT of class**

course give keep let's ~~starving~~

1 I'm *starving* !
2 ______ make an omelette.
3 Of ______ .
4 Can you ______ me a hand?
5 ______ an eye on it.

6 Complete the dialogues with phrases from Exercise 5. **OUT of class**

1 A: *I'm starving!*
 B: Me too! Can we eat now?
2 A: What can we cook?
 B: ______
3 A: ______
 B: Sure. What can I do?
4 A: The omelette is in the frying pan. ______
 B: No problem, but hurry up!
5 A: Can you cook eggs?
 B: ______ They're easy!

2.5 LISTENING and VOCABULARY | Shopping for food

I can identify specific detail in a conversation and talk about shopping for food.

1 Complete the names of the popular supermarket foods. What's the hidden word?

					[1] *b*	*e*	*a*	*n*	*s*
				[2]					
					o				
					w				
			[3]						
			[4]						
[5]									
					s				

1 baked ________
2 ice ________
3 fish ________
4 cheese and ________ crisps
5 chocolate chip ________
The hidden word is: ________ .

2 Complete the phrases with the words below.

about else idea let's much ~~on~~ price special

1 What's *on* the shopping list?
2 Good ________ .
3 Anything ________ ?
4 What ________ biscuits?
5 Right, ________ go!
6 It's a good ________ .
7 A ________ price today.
8 How ________ are the cookies?

3 07 Listen and tick the foods they must buy.

1 [ ] milk
2 [ ] butter
3 [ ] bread
4 [ ] eggs
5 [ ] cereal
6 [ ] yoghurts
7 [ ] fish fingers
8 [ ] ice cream
9 [ ] cheese
10 [ ] baked beans

4 Match prices 1–6 with how we say them (a–f).

1 [c] £15
2 [ ] 64p
3 [ ] 15p
4 [ ] £6.40
5 [ ] £7.50
6 [ ] 75p

a six pounds forty (pence)
b sixty-four p (pence)
c fifteen pounds
d fifteen p (pence)
e seventy-five p (pence)
f seven pounds fifty p (pence)

5 08 Listen and write the prices.

1 bananas: ________
2 cookies: ________
3 crisps: ________
4 brown bread: ________
5 white bread: ________

2.6 SPEAKING Ordering food

I can order food and drink.

1 Match photos A–H with words 1–8.

A B C D E F G H

1	D hot dog	5	risotto
2	kebab	6	curry
3	noodles	7	mineral water
4	soup	8	mint tea

2 Order the words to make phrases for ordering food and drink.

1 you / like / what / would / ?
What would you like?

2 chips / burger / please / with / a

3 please / a / me / for / sandwich / cheese

4 orange / have / can / please / juice / I / an / ?

5 else / anything / ?

6 that / all / is / ?

7 some / get / drinks / you / I / can / ?

8 you / are / here

9 OK / everything / is / ?

10 desserts / any / ?

11 £5.75 / please / that's

3 Write the phrases from Exercise 2 in the correct column. One phrase can go in both columns.

Waiter	Customer
What would you like?	

4 Complete the dialogues with phrases from the table in Exercise 3.

a A: [1]*What would you like?*
B: A cheese omelette, please.
A: [2] ______
B: Some chips and salad, please.

b A: [3] ______
B: Yes, please. Water for Liam. [4] ______
A: Of course. So that's water and orange juice. [5] ______
B: An ice cream for Liam, please.
A: Is that all?
B: Yes, thanks. No dessert for me.

c A: [6] ______
B: Yes, it's delicious! Thank you.

d A: How much is that?
B: [7] ______
A: Here you are.

5 Complete the dialogues with the words/phrases below. **OUT of class**

just joking never mind sure

1 A: I haven't got enough money to pay!
B: Oh no! What can we do?
A: ______! I've got the money!

2 A: Have you got any ketchup?
B: ______. Here you are.

3 A: It's closed!
B: ______. We can go tomorrow.

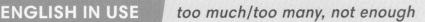

2.7 ENGLISH IN USE *too much/too many, not enough*

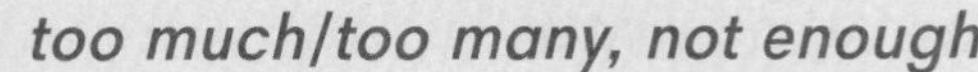

I can use *too much/too many* and *not enough* to talk about quantities.

1 Order the words to make sentences.

1 milk / there / coffee / enough / my / isn't / in
There isn't enough milk in my coffee.
2 much / tea / in / too / there's / sugar / my
______
3 got / glasses / haven't / enough / we
______
4 aren't / dinner / plates / there / for / enough
______
5 are / for / crisps / many / two / there / people / too
______
6 too / I've / burger / with / many / my / got / chips
______

2 Choose the correct answer.

1 There is too ___ milk in the glass.
(a) much b many c enough
2 There are too ___ fish fingers on my plate.
a much b many c enough
3 There aren't ___ biscuits for us.
a much b many c enough
4 There ___ enough cheese for an omelette.
a aren't b are c isn't
5 There are ___ many chips for me.
a very b lots c too
6 There ___ too much salt in the scrambled eggs.
a is b are c aren't

3 Complete the text with one or two words in each gap.

This meal [1]*isn't* very good for you. There are [2]______ many calories. There [3]______ too many chips and there [4]______ enough meat. There's too [5]______ salt in the sauce and [6]______ aren't enough vegetables. The dessert is ice cream. It's delicious but there's too [7]______ sugar in it. The meal is £20.00 and that's [8]______ much money!

4 Choose the correct option.

1 There are two *kilos* / (*litres*) of milk in the big bottle.
2 I've got a small *bottle* / *tin* of water in my bag for the journey.
3 Get two *litres* / *packets* of chocolate biscuits from the shop.
4 We haven't got any *tins* / *packets* of baked beans in the kitchen.
5 A *gram* / *kilo* of tomatoes is very expensive at the supermarket.
6 Put twenty-five *kilos* / *grams* of butter in the pan for the white sauce.

5 09 Complete the dialogue with one or two words in each gap. Listen and check.

Ann: OK. I've got the food for the barbecue today.
Ben: For [1]*how* many people?
Ann: About twenty-five.
Ben: What? That's [2]______ many! Our garden's [3]______ small.
Ann: Don't worry. It's OK.
Ben: Well, have you got [4]______ of food?
Ann: I've got ten big [5]______ of crisps and thirty hot dogs. Oh yes, and some hamburgers.
Ben: Mmm … And to drink?
Ann: There are fifteen small [6]______ of lemonade and ten [7]______ of cola.
Ben: That isn't [8]______ cola. What about [9]______ salad?
Ann: Yes, I've got four [10]______ of tomatoes and some celery. Oh, and three big onions for the hamburgers.
Ben: There [11]______ enough onions. And there are too [12]______ tomatoes. Have we got any bread for sandwiches? Maybe chicken?
Ann: Yes, we have. There isn't [13]______ chicken for chicken sandwiches. But we can have cheese and tomato sandwiches. Now [14]______ aren't too many tomatoes!
Ben: I can get some extra cola and onions.
Ann: No, we haven't got [15]______ time. Look, it's 3.30. And the barbecue is at 4.00!
Ben: Oh! I must start the sandwiches!

2.8 SELF-ASSESSMENT

For each learning objective, tick (✓) the box that best matches your ability.

☺☺ = I understand and can help a friend.

☺ = I understand and can do it by myself.

☹ = I understand but have some questions.

☹☹ = I do not understand.

		☺☺	☺	☹	☹☹	Need help?	Now try ...
2.1	Vocabulary					Students' Book pp. 22–23 Workbook pp. 18–19	Ex. 1–3, p. 27
2.2	Grammar					Students' Book p. 24 Workbook p. 20	Ex. 4, p. 27
2.3	Reading					Students' Book p. 25 Workbook p. 21	
2.4	Grammar					Students' Book p. 26 Workbook p. 22	Ex. 5, p. 27
2.5	Listening					Students' Book p. 27 Workbook p. 23	
2.6	Speaking					Students' Book p. 28 Workbook p. 24	Ex. 6, p. 27
2.7	English in use					Students' Book p. 29 Workbook p. 25	Ex. 5, p. 27

2.1 I can talk about food and drink.
2.2 I can use *there is/there are* to talk about places to eat in town.
2.3 I can find specific detail in a blog entry and talk about preparing food.
2.4 I can use countable and uncountable nouns to talk about quantities of food.
2.5 I can identify specific detail in a conversation and talk about shopping for food.
2.6 I can order food and drink.
2.7 I can use *too much/too many* and *not enough* to talk about quantities.

What can you remember from this unit?

New words I learned (the words you most want to remember from this unit)	**Expressions and phrases I liked** (any expressions or phrases you think sound nice, useful or funny)	**English I heard or read outside class** (e.g. from websites, books, adverts, films, music)

2.9 SELF-CHECK

Vocabulary

1 Complete the words.

1 Put this on your toast or bread: **b**_ _ _ _ _
2 Use these to make an omelette: **e**_ _ _
3 This red sauce is good on chips: **k**_ _ _ _ _ _
4 You can make wine from these: **g**_ _ _ _ _
5 Put this in coffee: **m**_ _ _
6 This is a nice and cold dessert: **i**_ _ **c**_ _ _ _
7 Buy these in a tin: **b**_ _ _ _ **b**_ _ _ _
8 Use this to fry food: **o**_ _

2 Match words 1–8 with words a–h.

1 a cheese	a cereal
2 a frying	b food
3 orange	c fingers
4 breakfast	d milkshake
5 a chocolate	e pan
6 a hot	f juice
7 fast	g dog
8 fish	h sandwich

3 Choose the correct answer.

1 Where's the ___ for my cereal?
a fork b plate c bowl
2 First, ___ the eggs in some water.
a boil b beat c fry
3 Don't put a lot of ___ on your food – it isn't good for you.
a milk b brownies c salt
4 ___ the bacon with the eggs.
a Boil b Fry c Cut
5 Can you help me ___ up the potatoes?
a cut b add c beat
6 Find some big ___ . There's a lot of food!
a forks b pepper c plates
7 We can ___ a cake for Jack's birthday.
a bake b fry c beat
8 Let's drink some ___ .
a crisps b cola c celery
9 Chocolate ___ cookies are my favourite.
a crisp b oil c chip
10 An ice cream, a bacon sandwich and a cheeseburger? Wow! That's a lot of ___ for dinner!
a peppers b calories c muffins

Grammar

4 Choose the correct option.

1 *There's / There are* a cake on the table for Gary.
2 *Is / Are* there any biscuits for me?
3 There isn't *a / any* frying pan, so we can't have fried eggs.
4 There are *some / any* glasses on the table and there's *some / any* juice in the fridge.
5 *Is / Are* there a good website for vegetarian recipes?
6 There *isn't / aren't* any sausages.

5 Complete the sentences with one or two words in each gap.

1 How _______ money have you got?
2 There isn't _______ cola in this glass.
3 How _______ people are at Tom's party?
4 Are there _______ cheese sandwiches? I can only see chicken ones.
5 There's _______ bottle of milk in the fridge. Can you get it, please?
6 There _______ many restaurants in our town – only two.
7 There are _______ bottles of cola – two, I think, but there isn't _______ lemonade.
8 There's _______ much ketchup on my chips. I can't eat them.
9 I haven't got _______ oil in the pan to fry three eggs.
10 There are a _______ of sausages to cook!

Speaking language practice

6 Match questions 1–6 with answers a–f.

1 ☐ What would you like?
2 ☐ Can I order a salad, please?
3 ☐ How much is that?
4 ☐ Is everything OK?
5 ☐ Any desserts?
6 ☐ Where's the salt?

a It's delicious.
b No, thanks.
c Here you are.
d Yes, of course.
e £5.50, please.
f Fish fingers and chips, please.

1 Order the letters and write the words in the sentences.

1 You can buy ***memorabilia*** (iailomrebam) to remember a special day or event.
2 You can give money to ________ (cathiry). It can help people.
3 Some children can't sleep in the ________ (rkad) and they've got a light in their rooms.
4 People can remember the ________ (eastt) of good, delicious food.
5 If you can sing and act, you can be in an ________ (rapoe).

2 Complete the sentences with the adjectives below.

blind royal special ~~traditional~~ unusual

1 A ***traditional*** meal in the UK is fish and chips.
2 4 November is a ________ day for me. It's my birthday.
3 It's very hot today. That's very ________ in January!
4 The ________ family have got a big palace in London.
5 My friend is ________ . She's got a clever dog to help her.

3 Find eight words from Exercises 1 and 2 in the word search. Look ↑, ↓, ↗ and ↘.

M	I	W	N	T	Y	F	B	J
Y	U	Q	O	A	O	D	S	F
D	C	R	K	S	P	E	P	R
C	Z	V	B	T	E	V	E	P
H	D	I	L	E	R	H	C	I
A	A	M	I	U	A	E	I	L
R	R	U	N	U	S	U	A	L
I	K	W	D	Y	T	Y	L	P
T	J	W	O	L	O	D	T	O
Y	P	R	Z	R	I	O	L	Z

4 Choose the correct option.

1 It's good to *(play)* / *serve* games with friends.
2 *Good* / *Happy* luck in the competition!
3 They *play* / *serve* good meals in this restaurant.
4 We can *move* / *cook* food in a pan.
5 Can you *steam* / *taste* dumplings in this bowl?
6 The Japanese can *serve* / *make* good cars.
7 There's a *black* / *scary* line on the floor.
8 I've got a *pink* / *science* fiction book.

5 Look at the pictures and complete the word puzzle. What's the hidden word?

			[1] *s*	*t*	*e*	*a*	*m*
2							
	3						
			4				
	5						
			6				
		7					

The hidden word is: ________ .

1

2

3

4

5

6

7
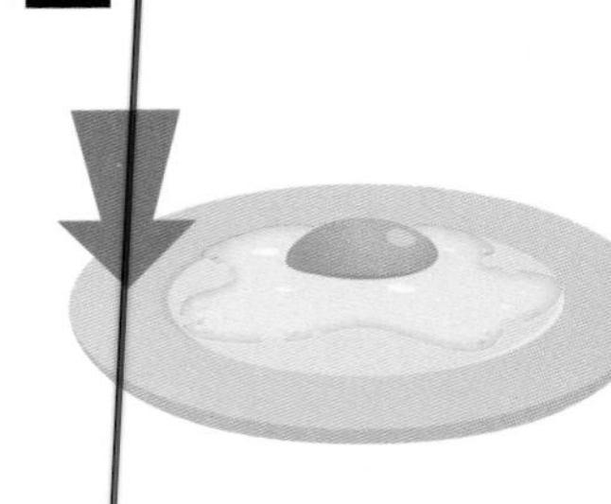

6 **Read the video script. Underline any words or phrases you don't know and find their meaning in your dictionary.**

Tomorrow's food

Robots can do many things. They can walk and talk. They can make cars and play games. We've got them in lots of places. But what about in a restaurant? Can robots serve food? And can they cook good meals? Is that too difficult for a robot or is it science fiction? No, it isn't. In China there's an unusual restaurant. It's got robot waiters. They can bring food to your table. There's a long black line on the floor and the robot waiters can move on it and stop at tables. The robots have got plates with the meals on and they've all got pretty pink and blue aprons. They can talk too. 'Good luck to you, my customer!' And who's this? It's a robot chef. This robot can cook. But it can't put the food on the plates. This is fun. Thank you, robot.

3.1 VOCABULARY Verbs to describe routines

I can talk about daily routines.

Every day

VOCABULARY
Verbs to describe routines | Verb collocations

GRAMMAR
Present Simple (affirmative and negative) | Present Simple (questions and short answers)

READING
Free time activities | Life at a language school in England

LISTENING
Feelings

SPEAKING
Likes and dislikes

WRITING
Daily routine

BBC CULTURE
Do child actors go to school every day?

EXAM TIME 1 > p. 114

1 ● Complete the time phrases with *in* or *at*.

1 *in* the morning
2 _____ the afternoon
3 _____ the evening
4 _____ night
5 _____ 8 p.m.

2 ● Look at the pictures and complete the phrases.

1 e*xercise*

2 r_ _ _ _

3 g_ _ u_

4 w_ _ _ u_

5 g_ h_ _ _

6 s_ _ _ _

7 h_ _ _ b_ _ _ _ _ _ _ _

8 w_ _ _

9 h_ _ _ a s_ _ _ _ _

10 g_ t_ b_ _

11 g_ t_ s_ _ _ _ _

12 h_ _ _ d_ _ _ _ _

3 ●● Complete the sentences with phrases from Exercise 2.

1 Every morning I *wake up* at 7.30.
2 I __________ at 7.35.
3 I __________ at 7.45. Then I get dressed and go downstairs.
4 I __________ with my parents at 8.00. Maybe toast or an egg.
5 I __________ by bus at 8.30. My lessons start at 9.00.
6 My parents __________ at my school – they're teachers!
7 Lessons finish at 4.00. I __________ by bus at 4.30.
8 I __________ at home before dinner. I read a book or watch TV.
9 I sometimes __________ at the gym after school.
10 I __________ with my family at 6.30.
11 I __________ after dinner. We have lots of homework.
12 By 9.30 I'm very tired and I __________ .

4 Look at the table. Complete the sentences below with *sometimes*, *often* or *never*.

	toast	eggs and bacon	cereal
Monday	✗	✗	✓
Tuesday	✗	✗	✓
Wednesday	✗	✗	✓
Thursday	✗	✗	✓
Friday	✗	✗	✓
Saturday	✗	✓	✗
Sunday	✗	✓	✗

1 I ______ have toast for breakfast.
2 I ______ have eggs and bacon for breakfast.
3 I ______ have cereal for breakfast.

5 WORD FRIENDS **Match verbs 1–5 with words/phrases a–e.**

1 [d] go a friends
2 [ ] meet/text b karate
3 [ ] check c homework/housework
4 [ ] do d to the cinema
5 [ ] do e my emails

6 **Complete the sentences with word friends from Exercise 5.**

1 I like films. I often *go to the cinema* with my friends.
2 My friends write a lot of emails. I ______ after every lesson.
3 I exercise a lot. I often ______ after school.
4 After school I sometimes ______ in the park.
5 After dinner I ______ in my room.

7 **Complete the crossword.**

Across
2 Not in the morning – in the ______ .
4 You can do this at the gym.
7 Help your mum with this.
8 Not sometimes but ______ .
10 Do this exercise to relax.
11 I ______ my friends on my phone.
12 I've got an alarm clock to help me ______ up.

Down
1 It's important to ______ before you go to bed, e.g. read a book.
3 I ______ my emails every hour.
5 I ______ a lot. I want to go to university.
6 Not often but ______ .
7 Our teacher gives us a lot of ______ .
9 I often ______ my friends to go shopping.

8 **Complete the text with one word in each gap.**

I'm Jenny Middleton. I'm a teacher. I [1]*wake* up at 7.30 and I [2]______ up five minutes later. I [3]______ a shower and then I [4]______ breakfast with my family. I [5]______ to work by car at 8.30. Lessons start at 9.15. I [6]______ lunch with the other teachers at 12.30. I [7]______ home at 4.30. I sometimes [8]______ after school at the gym – it's good for me! I have dinner with my husband and children at 6.30. I sometimes [9]______ some housework after dinner and then I [10]______ watch TV or read a book. I read my students' homework and [11]______ my emails before bed. I [12]______ go to bed before 12.00 – I'm a night owl!

Present Simple (affirmative and negative)

I can use the Present Simple to talk about habits.

1 Match photos A–E with words 1–5.

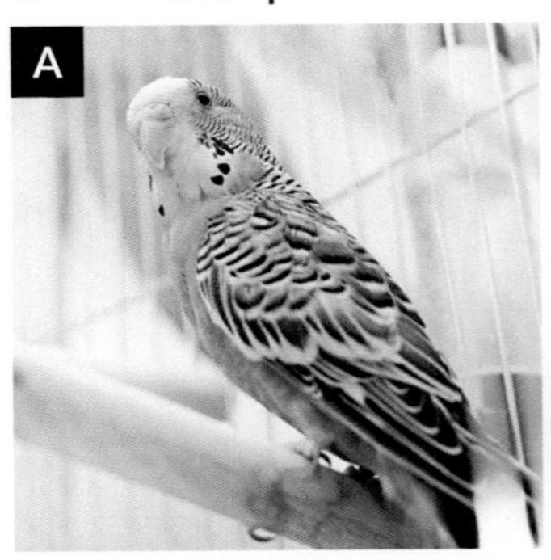
A

B

C

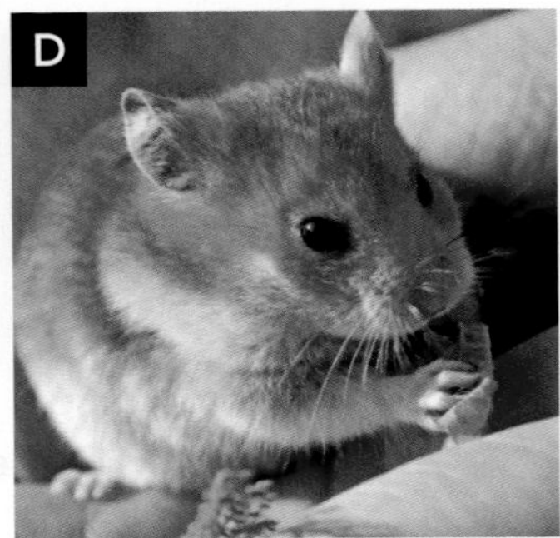
D

E

1 [*D*] hamster
2 [ ] pony
3 [ ] tortoise
4 [ ] budgie
5 [ ] guinea pig

2 Look at the endings of the verbs below. Which verbs have the same sound? Write them in the correct category.

~~checks~~ cries does exercises finishes gets goes has makes meets relaxes studies

1 /ɪz/: misses, ______ , ______ , ______
2 /z/: stays, ______ , ______ , ______ , ______ , ______
3 /s/: sleeps, *checks* , ______ , ______ , ______

3 Complete the sentences with the Present Simple form of the verbs in brackets.

1 I *have* (have) breakfast at 8.30.
2 We ______ (go) shopping at the weekend.
3 My brother ______ (spend) a lot of time on his computer in the evening.
4 Eva ______ (go) to the cinema every Saturday.
5 You ______ (get) good marks in English!
6 The teachers ______ (give) us lots of homework on Fridays.
7 My cousin ______ (have) a big lunch every day.

4 Make the sentences in Exercise 3 negative.

1 *I don't have breakfast at 8.30.*
2 ______
3 ______
4 ______
5 ______
6 ______
7 ______

5 Make sentences in the Present Simple.

1 I / like / pop music
I like pop music.
2 we / not have / English / on Mondays
______
3 my sister / not help / my mum / with the housework
______
4 our cat / not sleep / a lot
______
5 Mike / often / watch / TV / in the evening
______
6 you / never / eat / crisps
______
7 my friends / go / to yoga / on Thursdays
______

6 Complete the blog with the Present Simple form of the verbs below.

give go (x2) have (x2) like meet not eat not finish not see sleep visit

myblog

My pets, Tickle and Maxi

We [1]*have* two cats, Tickle and Maxi. Tickle is old and she [2]______ a lot, sometimes for hours and hours! She [3]______ much – she leaves nearly all her food – and never [4]______ out. Maxi is young and she [5]______ out every night. Sometimes we [6]______ her all day. I think she [7]______ her friends in the garden! She [8]______ dinner every evening at 5.30. She [9]______ fish and cat biscuits very much. Sometimes she starts but [10]______ her dinner. I think she [11]______ different houses and the people [12]______ her food too! She's a BIG cat!

I can find specific detail in an article and talk about free time activities.

1 WORD FRIENDS **Choose the correct option.**

1 I always listen (to) / *for* music in the car.
2 I sometimes *write* / *chat* with my friend in Australia online.
3 My dad usually browses *the internet* / *the TV* when he gets home from work.
4 My sister and I *do* / *play* cards a lot when we're on holiday.
5 We always *watch* / *look* sport on TV at the weekend.

2 Read the text. Match paragraphs 1–3 with headings a–d. There is one extra heading.

a ☐ Free time with friends
b ☐ Lesson time
c ☐ Home time
d ☐ Holiday time

3 Read the text again. Mark the sentences T (true) or F (false).

1 ☐ Nari sometimes speaks Korean to her English family.
2 ☐ Nari goes to school two days a week.
3 ☐ All students at the language school are Korean.
4 ☐ Nari only has lessons in the morning.
5 ☐ In class, Nari studies grammar.
6 ☐ The lessons are fun.
7 ☐ Nari does sports in the afternoons.
8 ☐ Nari meets other students at weekends.

4 Find words in the text that have these meanings.

1 You have this at night: **d***ream*
2 This is a journey where you go and come back in a short time: **t**_ _ _
3 You find the meaning of words in this: **d**_ _ _ _ _ _ _ _ _
4 This person tells you the meaning of something in another language: **t**_ _ _ _ _ _ _ _ _
5 You get this when you pass a test or finish a course: **c**_ _ _ _ _ _ _ _ _ _
6 This tells you about the ideas and the way of life in a country: **c**_ _ _ _ _ _

myblog

Life at a language school in England

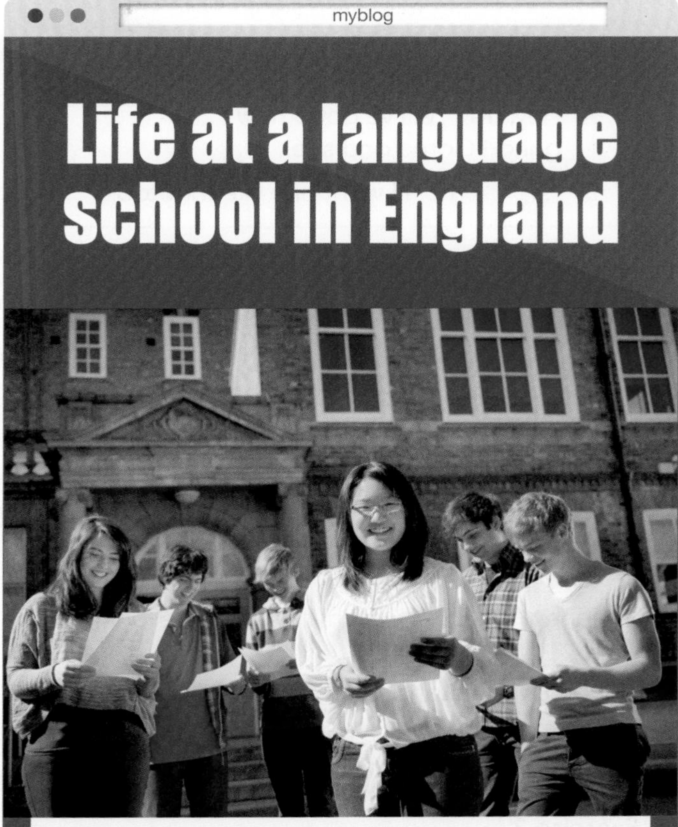

I'm Nari. I'm Korean, but English is an important language for me. I want to be a translator and I'm in England for six months at a language school. It's fantastic! I'm in a lovely town by the sea and I have a room with a very nice family. They speak English to me all the time. It's hard but very good for me. When I have breakfast, we speak English. When I watch TV, we speak English. I think I speak English in my dreams!

Every day I go to a language school and study English with students from different countries. We never speak our own language – only English. We have five lessons every day, from 9.30 to 4.30. We study difficult things like grammar but the teachers are cool and sometimes we sing English songs and play games in class. There's a lot of talking too. It isn't only books, books and books! But my dictionary is very useful! At the end of the course we get a certificate.

After lessons we often do sports or watch films at school, and at weekends I sometimes go on trips to interesting places with other students. I love this school. I have friends here from all over the world and learn about their cultures too. My best friend here is from Spain. It's a great life!

Present Simple (questions and short answers)

I can use the Present Simple to ask about routines.

1 Complete the words in the dialogue. OUT of class

A: Hey, [1]m_ _e! I've got a new guitar! Come and see.

B: [2]A_ _ _ _m_ ! I want one like that too!

2 ● Make questions in the Present Simple.

1 you / live / in London / ?
Do you live in London?
2 Pete / like / pop music / ?
______
3 we / have / a History test / every week / ?
______
4 Jo and Lee / go / to the cinema / on Saturday / ?
______
5 Jenny / always / watch / TV / in the evening / ?
______
6 you / understand / German / ?
______

3 ● Write short answers for the questions in Exercise 2.

1 ✓ *Yes, I do.*
2 ✗ ______
3 ✗ ______
4 ✓ ______
5 ✓ ______
6 ✗ ______

4 ●● Write questions for the answers. Use question words (*where*, *what*, *when*, *how*, etc.).

1 A: *What time do you go to school?*
B: I go to school at 8.30.
2 A: ______
B: I watch music programmes and films.
3 A: ______
B: I travel to town by bus.
4 A: ______
B: She goes swimming at the leisure centre.
5 A: ______
B: My mum and dad get up at 7.15.
6 A: ______
B: In my free time I do lots of sports.
7 A: ______
B: My brother works in Manchester.

5 ●● Find and correct the mistakes in the sentences. One sentence is correct.

1 Do James like celery?
Does James like celery?
2 Where does Mike plays football?
______
3 Does you have lunch at school?
______
4 A: Do you have any Spanish friends?
B: No, I doesn't.
______
5 How do you usually cook eggs?
______
6 What time do we finishes school on Monday?
______

6 ●●● Complete the dialogue with the words below.

do (x2) does don't I no speak ~~want~~ when where yes

A: Hi! You're a new student, aren't you? I'm Jenny. I'm in your class. Do you [1]*want* to ask me any questions?
B: Oh hi! Thanks, I've got lots! First, [2]______ do lessons stop for lunch?
A: Good question! We finish for lunch at 12.15 and start again at 1.00.
B: OK. [3]______ we have Maths lessons every day?
A: No, we [4]______ . Only on Mondays, Wednesdays and Fridays.
B: That's good! [5]______ do we do sports?
A: We do exercises in the gym and play team sports on the field.
B: And what about the teacher, Miss Masters? [6]______ she give a lot of homework?
A: [7]______ , she does! Loads!
B: Oh, dear! Thank you. By the way, I'm Emilio.
A: That's an Italian name. Are you Italian?
B: My dad's Italian and my mum's English. Do you [8]______ Italian?
A: [9]______ , I don't. But I can understand a little.
B: [10]______ you want to learn? I can teach you some.
A: Yes [11]______ do, Emilio. Thanks!

3.5 LISTENING and VOCABULARY Feelings

I can identify specific detail in a radio programme and talk about feelings.

1 Match the adjectives below with the pictures.

bored excited ~~happy~~ sad tired worried

1 *happy*

2 __________

3 __________

4 __________

5 __________

6 __________

2 Match 1–6 with a–f to make sentences.

1 [c] I feel excited
2 [ ] I feel bored
3 [ ] I feel sad
4 [ ] I feel tired
5 [ ] I feel worried
6 [ ] I feel relaxed

a when I've got a lot of homework and I haven't got much time.
b when my friends move away and I don't see them often.
c when it's nearly the holidays and I plan lots of things with my friends.
d when all my friends are busy and there aren't any good programmes on TV.
e when I haven't got any homework and I can sit down to read a good book and listen to music.
f when I go to bed too late and get up early for school.

3 10 Listen to a radio interview and choose the correct answer.

1 *A Happy Life* is
 a a radio programme.
 b a theatre play.
 c a book.
2 The interviewer is with
 a two actors.
 b three actors.
 c four actors.
3 The interview is about
 a what actors do before a play.
 b how actors feel after a play.
 c how actors learn words for a play.

4 10 Listen again. Match the speakers (1–4) with what they do before a play (a–f). There are two extra activities.

1 [ ] Liam
2 [ ] Debbie
3 [ ] Mark
4 [ ] Anna

a read a book
b walk a lot
c practise words
d eat sandwiches
e sleep
f listen to music

3.6 SPEAKING Talking about likes and dislikes

I can talk about likes and dislikes.

OUT of class

1 Replace two words in the sentences with *guy* and *a bit*.

1 I like learning Japanese. It's quite difficult but it's interesting.

____

2 Do you know the man over there? He wants to talk to us.

____

2 Order the words to make sentences and questions about likes and dislikes.

1 favourite / it's / my / !
It's my favourite!
2 think / do / Sam Smith / of / you / what / ?
3 you / Coldplay / like / do / ?
4 sad / love / films / watching / I
5 kind / like / books / you / what / do / of / ?
6 like / I / chocolate / really
7 a / like / lot / football / I
8 like / I / tennis / quite
9 mind / school / cycling / don't / to / I
10 don't / Adele / like / I
11 enjoy / I / Maths / don't
12 can't / onions / stand / I
13 like lemonade / I / but / prefer cola / I

3 Write the numbers of the sentences from Exercise 2 in the correct category.

1 ☺ *1,* ______
2 😐 ______
3 ☹ ______
4 ? ______

4 Complete the dialogues with one word in each gap.

1 A: What do you *think* of the new James Bond film?
B: I ______ like it. It's fantastic!
2 A: What ______ of books do you enjoy?
B: I ______ like funny books but I ______ exciting ones.
3 A: Do you like Chinese food?
B: It's my ______ !
4 A: Do you like Adele's new song?
B: I can't ______ it!
5 A: Do you like playing tennis?
B: I don't ______ it but I prefer playing volleyball.
6 A: Do you enjoy learning French?
B: Yes, I like it a ______ .

5 Find and correct the mistakes in the sentences. One sentence is correct.

1 I like James Bond quite.
I quite like James Bond.
2 What do you think for the new French restaurant?
3 I can't stand getting up early.
4 I quite like go to the cinema.
5 A: Do you like chicken?
B: I love him.

6 Choose the correct response.

1 What do you think of the new TV series?
a No, I can't stand TV.
(b) I quite like it.
c I like watching TV a lot.
2 What kind of music do you like?
a I don't mind it.
b I quite like it but I prefer hip-hop.
c I like hip-hop a lot.
3 Do you enjoy dancing?
a I prefer dancing.
b I really like singing.
c I hate it.
4 Do you like opera?
a I love them!
b I can't stand it.
c I quite like.

3.7 WRITING Describing daily routine

I can write about daily routine.

1 Complete the blog with the words below.

after (x2) at because (x2) do don't finish ~~it~~ lot so then (x2)

My day

I'm a swimmer. I love [1]*it*! A swimmer needs to do a [2]__________ of practice and my days are very busy, [3]__________ every morning I get up at 5.00 – yes, 5.00! I [4]__________ have a big breakfast but I drink a cup of tea. [5]__________ my dad takes me to the swimming pool. I get there [6]__________ 5.30 exactly. I train for two and a half hours. Then I have a shower and dad takes me home again. I have a big breakfast with the family at 8.30. [7]__________ that I cycle to school. Lessons [8]__________ at 4.30. [9]__________ I go swimming again for an hour and a half, from 4.45 to 6.15. [10]__________ swimming I go home and have dinner. I [11]__________ my homework in my room and then, at about 8.00, I watch some TV or play some computer games. I go to bed early, at 9.00, [12]__________ I'm tired and it's 5.00 again the next morning! I swim a lot [13]__________ I want to be a famous swimmer!

2 Read the blog again. Complete the table.

Time	Activity
5.00	[1]*get up*
[2]	arrive at swimming pool
[3]	finish training
8.30	[4]
4.30	[5]
4.45	[6]
[7]	finish swimming
8.00	[8]
9.00	[9]

3 Add the words in brackets to the sentences. Sometimes you need to join the sentences. Sometimes you need to change the order of the sentences.

1 I get up. I have a shower.
 a (then) *I get up. Then I have a shower.*
 b (after that) *I get up. After that I have a shower.*
 c (after) *After I get up, I have a shower.*

2 We have Maths. We have English.
 a (then) __________
 b (after that) __________
 c (after) __________

3 I have dinner. I play on my computer.
 a (then) __________
 b (after that) __________
 c (after) __________

4 I want to pass my exams. I work hard.
 a (so) *I want to pass my exams, so I work hard.*
 b (because) *I work hard because I want to pass my exams.*

5 I help my friend with her English homework. She isn't very good at English.
 a (so) __________
 b (because) __________

6 I live near my school. I walk to school in the morning.
 a (so) __________
 b (because) __________

4 Think of someone you know who has a different daily routine from you. Copy the table from Exercise 2 and complete it with information about him/her.

5 Write about the person's daily routine. Remember to do these things.

- Use your table from Exercise 4.
- Order the activities with *then*, *after that* and *after*.
- Give reasons with *so* and *because*.

3.8 SELF-ASSESSMENT

For each learning objective, tick (✓) the box that best matches your ability.

☺☺ = I understand and can help a friend.

☹ = I understand but have some questions.

☺ = I understand and can do it by myself.

☹☹ = I do not understand.

		☺☺	☺	☹	☹☹	Need help?	Now try ...
3.1	Vocabulary					Students' Book pp. 34–35 Workbook pp. 30–31	Ex. 1–3, p. 39
3.2	Grammar					Students' Book p. 36 Workbook p. 32	Ex. 4, p. 39
3.3	Reading					Students' Book p. 37 Workbook p. 33	
3.4	Grammar					Students' Book p. 38 Workbook p. 34	Ex. 5, p. 39
3.5	Listening					Students' Book p. 39 Workbook p. 35	
3.6	Speaking					Students' Book p. 40 Workbook p. 36	Ex. 6, p. 39
3.7	Writing					Students' Book p. 41 Workbook p. 37	

3.1 I can talk about daily routines.
3.2 I can use the Present Simple to talk about habits.
3.3 I can find specific detail in an article and talk about free time activities.
3.4 I can use the Present Simple to ask about routines.
3.5 I can identify specific detail in a radio programme and talk about feelings.
3.6 I can talk about likes and dislikes.
3.7 I can write about daily routine.

What can you remember from this unit?

New words I learned (the words you most want to remember from this unit)	**Expressions and phrases I liked** (any expressions or phrases you think sound nice, useful or funny)	**English I heard or read outside class** (e.g. from websites, books, adverts, films, music)

3.9 SELF-CHECK

Vocabulary

1 Choose the correct option.

1 I never *get* / *go* up early on Saturday.
2 After football Liam *has* / *does* a shower and then *goes* / *gets* home.
3 We *watch* / *look* TV every evening.
4 My parents *have* / *go* shopping after work on Wednesdays.
5 What time do you wake *out* / *up* in the morning?
6 Some people *look* / *check* their emails every hour.
7 My friends *do* / *make* yoga after school.
8 What kind of music do you listen *to* / *at*?
9 I often chat *at* / *with* my friends online.

2 Order the letters and write the words for pets in the sentences.

1 My gran has ________ (sdugebi). They're pretty little birds, yellow and green.
2 My friend has a ________ (shrmeat). It's small and brown and it runs a lot.
3 My sister wants a ________ (noyp). But my dad thinks it's too big and too expensive!
4 I'd like a ________ (stoorite). They're very slow and they live a long time!

3 Complete the sentences with the words below.

bored excited relaxed sad tired unhappy worried

1 It's my birthday and there's a party tonight. I'm very ________ .
2 This is a *long* walk! I'm ________ . Can we stop for a moment?
3 I've got bad test results and I'm ________ with them.
4 This song is very ________ . I always cry when I listen to it!
5 No school today! No homework! Cool! I'm very ________ !
6 I've got a test tomorrow. I can't remember my English verbs. I'm very ________ .
7 When there's nothing on TV and everyone is busy, I get ________ . So, I chat with my friends online.

Grammar

4 Complete the sentences with the Present Simple form of the verbs in brackets.

1 He never ________ (have) eggs for breakfast.
2 They ________ (not like) reading books.
3 I often ________ (exercise) in the gym after school.
4 My sister ________ (not relax) in the evening. She ________ (do) lots of homework.
5 We always ________ (speak) English in class.
6 I ________ (not go) to the cinema on Mondays.

5 Make questions in the Present Simple.

1 you / often / chat / with your friends online / ?
____
2 how much homework / your teacher / give / you / ?
____
3 when / your dad / go / to work / ?
____
4 where / you / have / lunch / at school / ?
____
5 what languages / your brother / speak / ?
____
6 how / your mum / get / to work / ?
____

Speaking language practice

6 Complete the sentences with the words below.

favourite hate kind mind of prefer quite stand

1 What ________ of music do you like?
2 I love chocolate cake. It's my ________ !
3 What do you think ________ the new TV show?
4 You're very tired. I don't ________ driving.
5 My friend can't ________ dogs. I don't know why!
6 I like tea but I ________ coffee. It's good to wake me up!
7 I ________ like watching football on TV but I ________ watching golf. It's very boring.

1 Match pictures A–F with words 1–6.

A
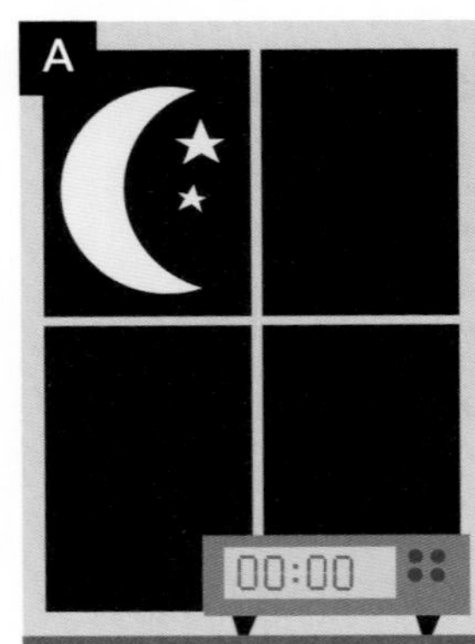

B

C

D

E

F

1 ☐ theatre
2 ☐ actor
3 ☐ show
4 ☐ midnight
5 ☐ burger
6 ☐ restaurant

2 Complete the words in the sentences.

1 A show in the afternoon is called a m*ati*n*ée*.
2 My friends go to a club and learn to a_ _. They are in a show next month.
3 I'm not very l_ _ _y. I never win competitions!
4 When I go on holiday, I m_ _s my friends.
5 No, this phone isn't the same as my phone – it's d_f_e_ _ _t.
6 I have a lot of homework today – there isn't much time to r_ _ _x.

3 Complete the sentences with words from Exercises 1 and 2.

1 We sometimes go to a *matinée* at the cinema on Saturday afternoons.
2 It's late and I'm very tired. Look at the time – it's __________!
3 My teacher wants me to __________ in the school play!
4 Does your brother __________ you and your family when he's away at university?
5 There's a new __________ in our town. Do you want to go there and see a show?
6 My grandfather is an __________. You can see him in lots of films.

4 Match 1–6 with a–f to make word friends.

1 [c] wake
2 ☐ go
3 ☐ do
4 ☐ make
5 ☐ act
6 ☐ miss

a your friends
b the cleaning
c someone up
d to a club
e in a show
f the breakfast

5 Order the letters and write the words in the sentences.

1 My friend Ben isn't free on Friday afternoons. He goes to a *club* (bcul).
2 Katy isn't at school today because she's __________ (lil).
3 Child actors don't have a __________ (ralnom) life. They do different things every day.
4 There's a lot of __________ (bribhus) on the beach. We must help clean it!
5 My mum is always __________ (ybsu) in the evening. She doesn't have time to watch TV.

6 Complete the sentences with the Present Simple form of the verbs in brackets.

1 My dad *sings* (sing) in the car.
2 My uncle __________ (not act) in a theatre. He __________ (act) in films.
3 I __________ (not do) the cleaning but I __________ (put out) the rubbish.
4 I often __________ (play) with my friends after school.
5 My mum __________ (relax) after dinner and __________ (watch) television.
6 Tina often __________ (help) her mum with the housework.

7 **Read the video script. Underline any words or phrases you don't know and find their meaning in your dictionary.**

A typical day?

What does a typical day of a school child look like? Do children around the world do the same things? Let's see! In the morning, they get up, wash their face, brush their teeth, and have breakfast. Then they go to school. Some take the bus, some walk, and some go by car. School is hard work everywhere, and there are different subjects for the students to learn. But school can be fun too and they can play with their friends in the breaks. After school, there is time to meet friends and family, play, relax, go to clubs and do sports. Some children help their parents with the housework. They help with shopping and preparing food. At the end of the day, it is time to have dinner and to go to bed. So, do children in different countries do the same things? Yes! Hmm, or maybe not?

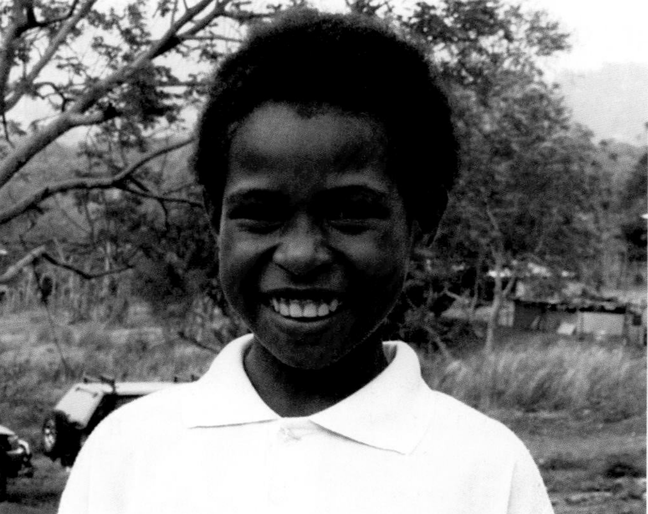

4 Love to learn

VOCABULARY
Classroom objects | School subjects

GRAMMAR
Present Continuous | Present Continuous and Present Simple

READING
School days

LISTENING
School life

SPEAKING
Polite requests

ENGLISH IN USE
Prepositions of place

BBC CULTURE
Can students learn without a timetable or classroom?

4.1 VOCABULARY School

I can talk about classroom objects and school subjects.

1 Match photos A–H with words 1–8.

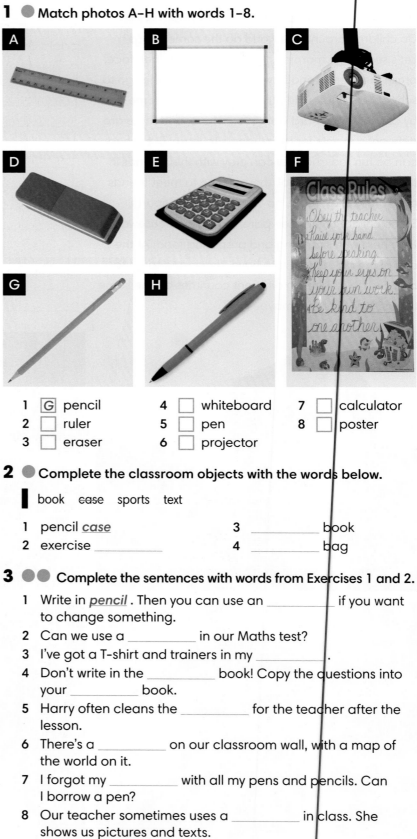

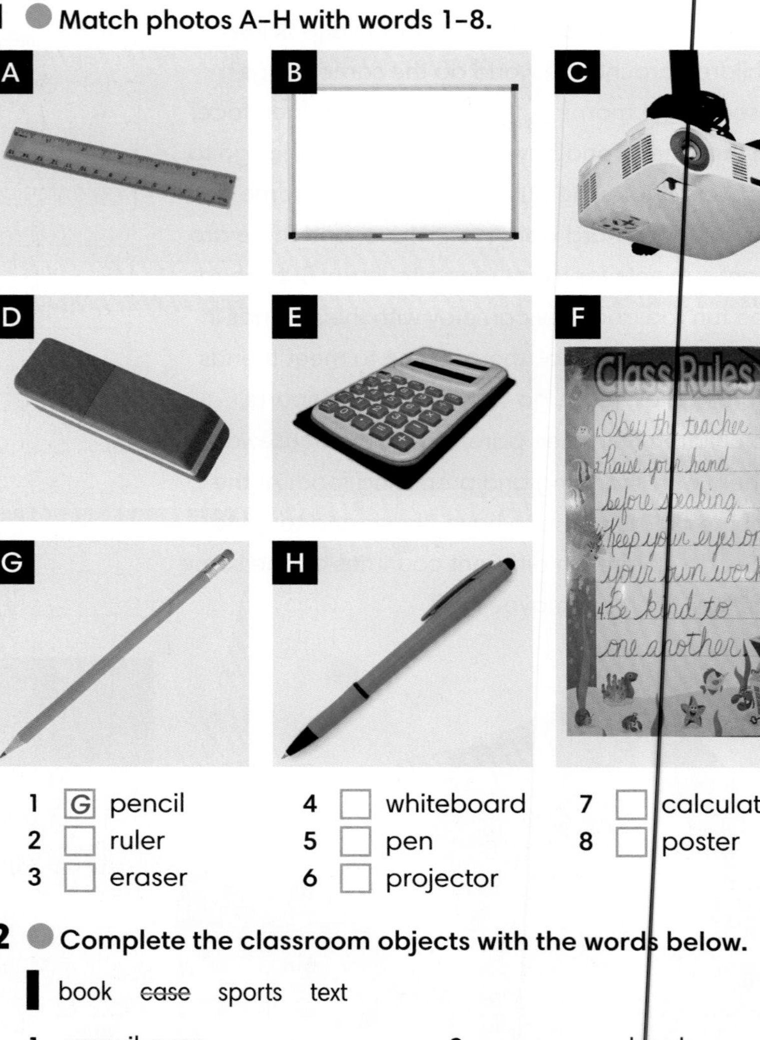

1 [G] pencil
2 [ ] ruler
3 [ ] eraser
4 [ ] whiteboard
5 [ ] pen
6 [ ] projector
7 [ ] calculator
8 [ ] poster

2 Complete the classroom objects with the words below.

book ~~case~~ sports text

1 pencil *case*
2 exercise ______
3 ______ book
4 ______ bag

3 Complete the sentences with words from Exercises 1 and 2.

1 Write in *pencil*. Then you can use an ______ if you want to change something.
2 Can we use a ______ in our Maths test?
3 I've got a T-shirt and trainers in my ______.
4 Don't write in the ______ book! Copy the questions into your ______ book.
5 Harry often cleans the ______ for the teacher after the lesson.
6 There's a ______ on our classroom wall, with a map of the world on it.
7 I forgot my ______ with all my pens and pencils. Can I borrow a pen?
8 Our teacher sometimes uses a ______ in class. She shows us pictures and texts.

4 Complete the school subjects.

1 Art
2 G_ _g_ _ _h_
3 B_ _l_g_
4 _i_t_r_
5 _ _gl_ _h
6 _a_hs
7 P_y_ _c_
8 M_ _i_
9 Dr_ _a
10 C_ _m_s_ _y

5 Find eight school subjects from Exercise 4 in the word search. Look ↑, ↓, ↗ and ↘.

O	J	M	C	C	K	I	A	A	A	O
A	H	E	N	M	E	R	L	S	R	L
F	H	D	M	O	L	S	Q	E	E	D
F	M	R	B	U	C	H	Y	R	N	M
N	A	A	M	I	S	R	I	Z	G	N
D	C	R	S	H	O	I	T	M	L	Q
U	R	Y	T	T	B	L	C	S	I	D
X	H	A	S	H	A	N	O	I	S	N
P	M	I	M	I	K	I	O	G	H	N
I	H	N	D	A	E	N	D	S	Y	E
M	N	U	N	Q	I	S	Q	H	T	Z

6 Match 1–4 with a–d to make school subjects.

1 [d] Information
2 [ ] Religious
3 [ ] Presentation
4 [ ] P

a Education
b Skills
c E
d Technology

7 Choose the correct option.

1 In (Geography) / *Maths* we look at maps of different countries.
2 *IT* / *PE* is fun because I love computers.
3 We learn about kings and queens in *History* / *Biology* and that's boring.
4 I'd like to be an actor, so *Drama* / *Physics* is my favourite subject.
5 We often go on holiday to different countries, so *Chemistry* / *English* is useful for me.
6 I can't paint or draw, so *Music* / *Art* is very difficult for me!
7 My dad's a doctor and he helps me with my *Religious Education* / *Biology* homework.

8 Choose the correct answer.

1 Are there any ___ on your classroom wall?
a rulers (b) posters c projectors
2 In our Geography ___ book there are some pictures of rivers in Africa.
a text b exercise c art
3 In ___ we sometimes copy songs into our exercise books and sing them.
a Physics b History c Music
4 The teacher shows us how to use ___ in our Presentation Skills class.
a a poster b a projector c an eraser
5 I like using ___ in Art classes because I can correct my mistakes.
a pencils b pens c a calculator
6 I forgot my sports ___ . It's in my bedroom at home!
a bag b case c ruler
7 If you use the wrong pen on the ___ , you can't clean it!
a projector b textbook c whiteboard

9 Complete the email with the words below.

Art breaks calculator erasers lessons Music PE pencil case subject ~~timetable~~

To: mia@fastmessage.com

Hi Mia,

My new school is great and this term's [1]*timetable* isn't bad. [2]__________ start at 9.00 and the first lesson on a Monday is [3]__________ ! Fantastic! You know I love painting. We've got [4]__________ on Tuesday morning and we learn to play the guitar – amazing! Wednesday isn't very good – we've got [5]__________ all afternoon. I hate sports and it always rains on Wednesdays! We have three [6]__________ every day – not two like our old school. It's good to chat to friends then.

Thanks for my present. It's a really pretty [7]__________ and I keep all my pens and [8]__________ in it. I've got a new [9]__________ too, to help with my Maths – not my favourite [10]__________ !

Write soon,
Steph

Present Continuous

I can use the Present Continuous to talk about things happening now.

1 ● **Look at the pictures and complete the sentences. Use the Present Continuous form of the verbs below. Use full forms.**

cry do yoga laugh listen to music ~~read~~ sleep smile walk

1 They *are reading*.

2 I ______________.

3 We ______________.

4 She ______________.

5 He ______________.

6 She ______________.

7 You ______________.

8 It ______________.

2 ● **Write the short forms of the verbs in Exercise 1.**

1 *They are = They're*
2 ______________
3 ______________
4 ______________
5 ______________
6 ______________
7 ______________
8 ______________

3 ● **Make the sentences in Exercise 1 negative.**

1 *They aren't reading.*
2 ______________
3 ______________
4 ______________
5 ______________
6 ______________
7 ______________
8 ______________

4 ● **Order the words to make questions.**

1 it / raining / is / ?
Is it raining?
2 TV / what / watching / are / you / on / ?
____
3 working / is / today / dad / your / ?
____
4 a / students / are / doing / test / the / ?
____
5 Hannah / is / running / why / ?
____
6 is / at / subject / sister / which / university / your / studying / ?
____

5 ●● **Match the questions in Exercise 4 with answers a–f.**

a [5] Because she's late.
b [ ] No, it isn't.
c [ ] Yes, they are.
d [ ] A new film.
e [ ] Maths.
f [ ] Yes, he is.

6 ●●● **Complete the phone conversation with the Present Continuous form of the verbs in brackets.**

Andy: Hi! What [1]*are you doing* (you/do)? [2]______________ (you/watch) TV?
Ben: No, [3]______________ (I/not). I [4]______________ (do) my Geography homework. It's horrible! How about you?
Andy: I [5]______________ (not do) any homework. I [6]______________ (listen) to some music. My mum [7]______________ (cook) dinner. I'm very hungry!
Ben: What [8]______________ (she/cook)?
Andy: Sausages. Lovely! I can smell them. And my dad [9]______________ (make) dessert: pancakes!
Ben: I [10]______________ (feel) hungry now!

I can find specific detail in a short story and talk about making friends.

1 WORD FRIENDS **Choose the correct option.**

1 My *first* / *(best)* friend is called Alice.
2 It's difficult to *get* / *go* to know people when you move to a new town.
3 I'm always shy when I meet someone *on* / *for* the first time.
4 It's good to *make* / *do* friends with people who like the same things as you.

2 Read the story below. Choose the best title.

a A night at Robby's house
b Robby's garden
c Tom's homework

3 Read the story again. Complete gaps 1–4 with sentences a–e. There is one extra sentence.

a Who is he speaking to?
b Now I understand.
c We've got homework every evening.
d Don't smile, boy.
e Tonight I'm staying with him but something strange is happening.

4 Find words in the story that have these meanings.

1 You do this when you are happy or when you like something: s_ _ _ _
2 Two students that are in the same class: c_ _ _ _ _ _ _ _ _
3 If something is not open, it is c_ _ _ _ _ .
4 A place in a house with flowers and trees: g_ _ _ _ _
5 You sleep in this at night: b_ _
6 When something makes us feel surprised or when we can't explain it, we say that it is s_ _ _ _ _ _ _ .

5 Read the story again. Mark the sentences ✓ (right), ✗ (wrong) or ? (doesn't say).

1 ☐ Tom and Robby live in the same town.
2 ☐ Tom and Robby are in different bedrooms.
3 ☐ It's nearly morning.
4 ☐ Tom is surprised.
5 ☐ Robby is talking to Tom.
6 ☐ Robby is still sleeping.

I'm Tom Stirling, and Robby Jones is my best friend. We're at the same school – we're classmates. I sometimes stay with Robby and I sleep in a bed in his room. [1]___ It's one o'clock in the morning but Robby isn't sleeping. He's standing by the window. The moon is shining. Robby is looking into the garden and he's speaking. What is he doing? [2]___ Now he's walking out of the room and I'm following him. Where's he going?

We're in the kitchen and Robby's sitting at the table. His eyes are closed but he's talking again. 'Where's your homework, Robby Jones? [3]___ I'm not laughing. I want your homework. Now!' Robby is speaking but the words are our teacher's!

Robby's standing up and going back to his room. He's walking past me but he can't see me. [4]___ He's walking and talking in his sleep!

Present Continuous and Present Simple

I can talk about what usually happens and what is happening now.

1 Complete the sentences with the words below.

OUT of class

lucky ready wow

1 The taxi's here. Are you __________ ?
2 What a lovely birthday present. You're really __________ !
3 __________ ! I've got 100 percent correct in my Maths test!

2 Mark the sentences N (now) or R (regular).

1 *R* I usually have a shower before breakfast.
2 [ ] My dad always drives to work.
3 [ ] Katy is swimming at the moment.
4 [ ] Pete is waiting for me at the bus stop.
5 [ ] We don't have dinner at 6.30 at the weekend.
6 [ ] My sister sometimes plays games on her computer.

3 Complete the sentences with the Present Simple or Present Continuous form of the verbs in brackets.

1 I usually *have* cereal for breakfast but today I *'m having* eggs and toast. (have)
2 Lindy usually __________ black clothes but today she __________ a yellow dress. (wear)
3 My dad usually __________ in town but today he __________ at home. (work)
4 My friends usually __________ for me outside school but today they __________ for me in the park. (wait)
5 Mum usually __________ films on TV but today she __________ a music competition. (watch)
6 We usually __________ English from a textbook but today we __________ an English song. (learn)

4 Make questions in the Present Simple or Present Continuous.

1 A: *Where do you live?*
(where / you / live / ?)
B: In Baker Street.
2 A: __________
(what / you / read / ?)
B: My new book.
3 A: __________
(Kenny / like / Chinese food / ?)
B: Oh, yes!
4 A: __________
(where / Jim / go / ?)
B: To his French class. He's late.
5 A: __________
(what / the teacher / write / ?)
B: Some sentences in the Present Simple.
6 A: __________
(Mark and Angela / study / French / on Fridays / ?)
B: No, on Thursdays.

5 Find and correct seven mistakes in the dialogue.

Sam: Hi, Liz. Do you come shopping with us? We want to buy some T-shirts.
Liz: Oh, yes! I don't often go clothes shopping. And I'm not having got many T-shirts.
Sam: We're usually going to the shopping mall but today we're going to the new shop in the High Street.
Liz: Cool! My sister is buying all her clothes there. She is working there every Saturday. She's saying that it's really good.
Sam: Does she work many hours there?
Liz: No, only mornings. Today's Friday, so she doesn't work now.

1 *Are you coming shopping with us?*
2 __________
3 __________
4 __________
5 __________
6 __________
7 __________

I can identify specific detail in a radio programme and talk about boarding schools.

1 WORD FRIENDS **Complete phrases 1–5 with the verbs below. Match them with pictures A–E.**

do ~~go~~ have revise start

1 [B] *go* to school
2 [ ] _____ school
3 [ ] _____ for exams
4 [ ] _____ homework
5 [ ] _____ classes

A

B

C

D

E

2 11 **Listen to the first part of a radio programme about a school. Choose the correct answer.**

The school is:

a only a boarding school.
b a school for boarders and day students.
c a girls' school.

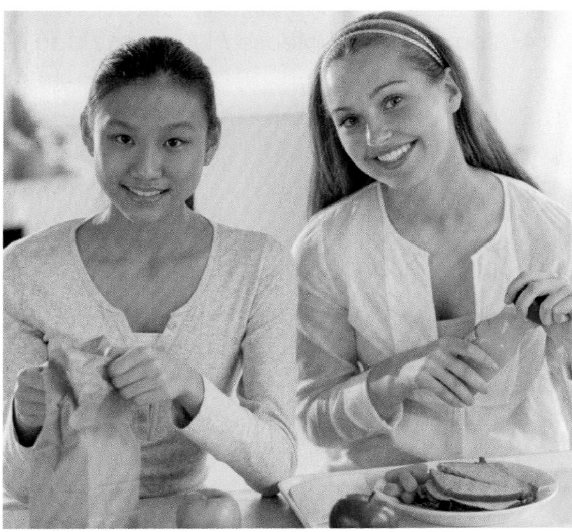

3 12 **Listen to the whole programme. Complete the sentences.**

Park Street School

1 There are _____ students at the school.
2 The students are aged from _____ to _____.
3 The school is _____ years old.
4 There are _____ boarders at the school.
5 Ella and Dixie are in Year _____.
6 They don't have classes on _____ afternoons.
7 Katherine's old teacher is called Miss _____.

4 12 **Listen again. Mark the sentences T (true) or F (false).**

1 [ ] It's Katherine's first visit to the school.
2 [ ] Katherine is in a classroom.
3 [ ] Ella revises at home.
4 [ ] Ella's house is quiet for revising.
5 [ ] Dixie likes playing tennis.
6 [ ] Ella wants to be a boarder.

I can make and respond to polite requests.

1 **Order the words to make polite requests and responses.**

1 borrow / eraser / I / your / can / ?
Can I borrow your eraser?
2 can't / you / sorry,
____
3 it / I / sorry, / need
____
4 some / have / please / I / water, / can / ?
____
5 no / yes, / problem
____
6 tell / can / number / your / me / phone / you / ?
____
7 just / second / OK, / a
____
8 help / computer / with / can / my / you / me / ?
____
9 course / yes, / of
____
10 it / I'm / sorry, / using
____

2 **Complete the sentences with one word in each gap.**

1 I've got a problem. *Can* you help me?
2 Hello, Doctor. Can ________ look at my hand, please?
3 OK, ________ a second. I want to finish this exercise.
4 Can you ________ me the time, please?
5 Yes, of ________ . Wait one moment.
6 A: Can ________ borrow your pen?
B: Sorry, I ________ it. Ask Tina.
7 Can I ________ a cheese sandwich, please?

3 **Match requests 1–5 with responses a–e.**

1 [e] My computer's got a problem. Can you help me?
2 [ ] Can I borrow your dictionary, please?
3 [ ] Can I have another glass of orange juice, please?
4 [ ] Can you tell me the answers, please?
5 [ ] Can I look at your dad's new car?

a Sure. That's £1.50
b Yes, OK. It's outside.
c Sorry, I can't. It's a test!
d Sorry, I need it.
e Of course I can. Where is it?

4 **Choose the correct response.**

1 Can you help me with my Geography homework?
a Sorry, I need it.
b Sorry, you can't.
(c) Sorry, I'm busy.
2 Can I borrow your phone for a moment?
a Yes, you can't.
b Yes, no problem.
c Yes, I'm using it.
3 Can you tell me the time, please?
a Sorry, I haven't got a watch.
b Yes, of course. It's there.
c Sure, it's lunchtime.
4 Can I have some ice cream, please?
a Sorry, you can't. There isn't any.
b Yes, OK. I can.
c Sorry, I can't.
5 Can I look at your exercise book?
a Yes, no problem.
b Yes, I can.
c Yes, I need it.

5 13 **Complete the dialogue with sentences a–e. Listen and check.**

Sal: It's Danny's party tonight. Can I borrow your blue shoes?
Mia: 1 ______
Sal: Can I borrow the red ones?
Mia: 2 ______
Sal: Can you help me with my hair? I can't see the back.
Mia: 3 ______
Sal: Hair, please!
Mia: 4 ______
Sal: Can you hurry up? I don't want to be late.
Mia: 5 ______
Sal: Yes, OK. Sorry.

a OK, just a second. They're in my sister's room. She likes the red ones too!
b OK, no problem. Can you sit down? Then I can look.
c Sorry, you can't. I'm wearing them.
d Sorry, I can't. Your hair is a mess. Sit still!
e Sorry, I can't do two things at the same time. Shoes or hair?

Prepositions of place

I can use prepositions of place to describe position.

1 **Look at the pictures and write the prepositions.**

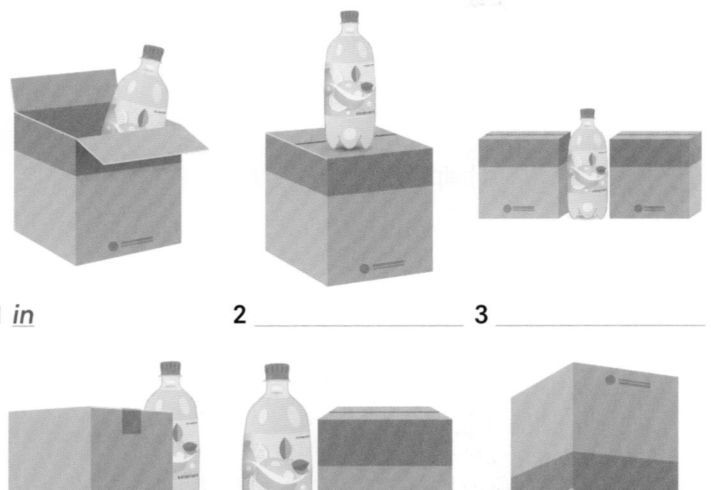

1 *in* 2 ______ 3 ______

4 ______ 5 ______ 6 ______

2 **Where are they? Look at the pictures and make sentences.**

1 textbook / bag
The textbook is in the bag.

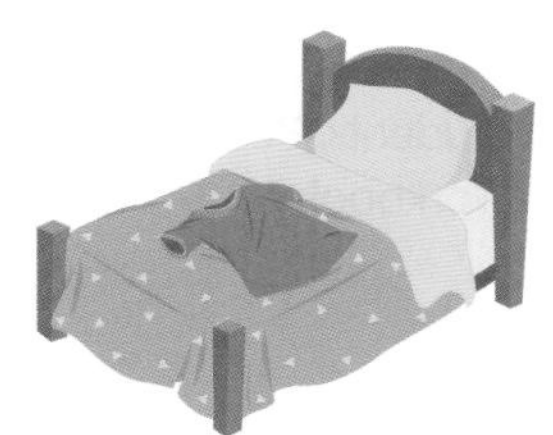

2 T-shirt / bed
______

3 girl / her parents
______

4 apple / banana
______

5 cat / dog
______

6 Eva / tree
______

3 **Find and correct the mistakes in the sentences.**

1 A: Where's Hannah?
B: She's on the classroom.
She's in the classroom.

2 Mum's putting the scrambled eggs in the plate now.
______

3 The teacher is behind the whiteboard. She's writing some questions.
______

4 A: I can't remember. What's behind your desk and your bed in your room?
B: There are some books on a shelf.

5 Go between me for the photo. You're very tall!
______

6 A: Have you got my magazine?
B: No, it's in front of the cat! The cat is sitting on it!
______

4 **Complete the dialogues with prepositions.**

A

Nick: Hi, Ted. I'm looking for Billy's house. Do you know it?

Ted: Yes, I do. It's number 18. At the moment we're standing [1]*in front of* number 2. Walk on for one minute and Billy's house is [2]______ a café and a shop. There are lots of roses [3]______ the garden! The shop [4]______ it is a cake shop!

B

Mum: Where's Helen?

Dan: She's playing a game with Adam. He's hiding [5]______ the tree and she can't find him.

Mum: Well, tell her that her dinner is [6]______ the table.

C

Mia: Look at the big boat [7]______ the bridge. It's my uncle's.

Kim: Lovely! I like standing [8]______ that bridge and looking down at the river and the boats.

4.8 SELF-ASSESSMENT

For each learning objective, tick (✓) the box that best matches your ability.

☺☺ = I understand and can help a friend.

☺ = I understand and can do it by myself.

☹ = I understand but have some questions.

☹☹ = I do not understand.

		☺☺	☺	☹	☹☹	Need help?	Now try ...
4.1	Vocabulary					Students' Book pp. 46–47 Workbook pp. 42–43	Ex. 1–3, p. 51
4.2	Grammar					Students' Book p. 48 Workbook p. 44	Ex. 4, p. 51
4.3	Reading					Students' Book p. 49 Workbook p. 45	
4.4	Grammar					Students' Book p. 50 Workbook p. 46	Ex. 5, p. 51
4.5	Listening					Students' Book p. 51 Workbook p. 47	
4.6	Speaking					Students' Book p. 52 Workbook p. 48	Ex. 7, p. 51
4.7	English in use					Students' Book p. 53 Workbook p. 49	Ex. 6, p. 51

4.1 I can talk about classroom objects and school subjects.
4.2 I can use the Present Continuous to talk about things happening now.
4.3 I can find specific detail in a short story and talk about making friends.
4.4 I can talk about what usually happens and what is happening now.
4.5 I can identify specific detail in a radio programme and talk about boarding schools.
4.6 I can make and respond to polite requests.
4.7 I can use prepositions of place to describe position.

What can you remember from this unit?

New words I learned (the words you most want to remember from this unit)	**Expressions and phrases I liked** (any expressions or phrases you think sound nice, useful or funny)	**English I heard or read outside class** (e.g. from websites, books, adverts, films, music)

4.9 SELF-CHECK

Vocabulary

1 Complete the words for classroom objects.

1 The teacher writes on this: **w**_ _ _ _ _ _ _ _ _
2 You can do Maths on this: **c**_ _ _ _ _ _ _ _ _
3 You can correct mistakes in your writing with this: **e**_ _ _ _ _
4 You keep things for writing in this: **p**_ _ _ _ _ **c**_ _ _
5 You write answers in this book: **e**_ _ _ _ _ _ _ **b**_ _ _
6 You learn subjects from this book: **t**_ _ _ **b**_ _ _
7 You put this on the wall in your classroom: **p**_ _ _ _ _
8 You use this to make lines: **r**_ _ _ _

2 Match the comments with the subjects below.

Art Biology English Geography History IT Maths PE

1 'Where is Japan?' ______
2 'I haven't got enough paint.' ______
3 'What's 156 x 72?' ______
4 'Why is Henry VIII famous?' ______
5 'We're learning to write a program.' ______
6 'This part of the eye is called the iris.' ______
7 'We use the Present Simple for routines.' ______
8 'Oh! I haven't got my football shorts.' ______

3 Complete the sentences with one verb in each gap.

1 I never ______ my homework before dinner.
2 My friends ______ to school by train.
3 We ______ classes from 9.30 to 4.30.
4 My brother and his best friend ______ for their exams together.
5 In my country children ______ school when they're five years old.

Grammar

4 Complete the sentences with the Present Continuous form of the verbs below.

go have laugh not work talk wear

1 I ______ because this story is very funny.
2 Who ______ (you) to on the phone? Is it Marcus?
3 Dad's worried because my brother ______ very hard at school at the moment.
4 ______ (Harry and Pete) to town on the bus?
5 ______ (Tom) new trainers? I really like them.
6 Ann ______ a driving lesson at the moment.

5 Choose the correct option.

1 We *have* / *are having* three Geography lessons every week. Today we *look* / *are looking* at mountains in France.
2 You *don't need* / *aren't needing* an umbrella. It *doesn't rain* / *isn't raining* at the moment.
3 I usually *work* / *am working* in London but today I *work* / *am working* on my computer at home.
4 My sister often *paints* / *is painting* pictures of our family. Right now she *paints* / *is painting* a picture of my mum.
5 Hi! No, I *don't do* / *am not doing* my homework. I *talk* / *am talking* to you on the phone!

6 Complete the sentences with prepositions.

1 The pens are ______ my pencil case. And my pencil case is ______ my desk so I can use it in this lesson.
2 Hannah sits ______ me in class. I can't see her, but I can hear her!
3 We always sit in pairs in class. Paul sits ______ Grant and Jacky sits ______ me.
4 The teacher is usually ______ us so we can see her.
5 We've got three posters on the wall. The one of the moon is ______ a poster of the stars and a poster of the planet Jupiter.

Speaking language practice

7 Complete the dialogues with one word in each gap.

1 A: ______ you help me with this History quiz?
B: No, ______, I can't.
2 A: Can I ______ your eraser?
B: ______ problem. Here you are.
3 A: Can I use your phone? Sorry! Mine's at home!
B: Of ______ you can. No worries!
4 A: Can you tell ______ Helen's phone number?
B: OK, ______ a second. It's on my phone.

1 Match pictures A–F with words 1–6.

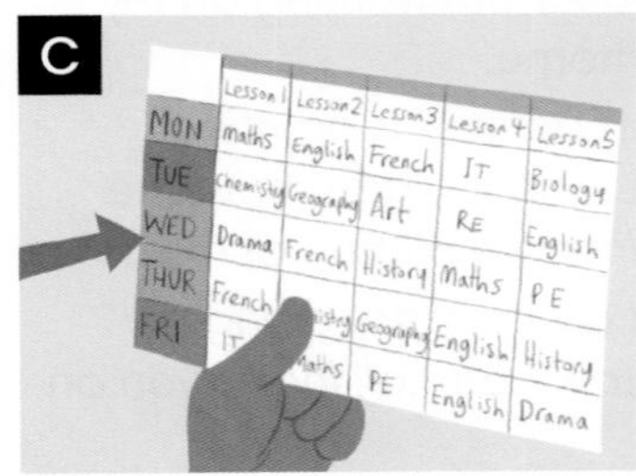

1 [*F*] furniture
2 [ ] rules
3 [ ] meeting
4 [ ] timetable
5 [ ] chair
6 [ ] desk

2 Complete the sentences with the words below.

choose decide lie make talk ~~work~~

1 I usually do my homework alone, but sometimes my friends and I *work* together.
2 Mum is feeling ill and she wants to ______ down.
3 Let's ______ a film: do you want to see *Henry* or *The Match?*
4 My friend doesn't ______ about his problems.
5 Our teachers ______ what goes on the timetable.
6 Students don't ______ rules in our school. It's the teachers.

3 Read the descriptions and complete the words.

1 A person in the same class as you: c*l a s s m a* te
2 Children play here: p_ _ _ _ _ _ _ _d
3 This school is for young children: p_ _ _ _ _y school
4 A country's food, music, special clothes, etc. are part of this: c_ _ _ _ _e
5 When you feel happy or hear a funny story, you do this: l_ _ _h

4 Complete the crossword.

Across

5 This isn't funny! Don't ______ !
6 I must buy new ______ for my room: a chair, a desk and a bed.
7 'Don't eat food in the classroom,' is a ______ .

Down

1 The teachers are having a *meeting* to decide what must go on the timetable.
2 My school has a big ______ for us to play in.
3 Traditional music is part of a country's ______ .
4 Sheila is very ______ – she has lots of ideas.

5 Complete the sentences with the Present Simple or Present Continuous form of the verbs in brackets.

1 They *aren't playing* (not play) in the playground at the moment. They ______ (have) a lesson.
2 The students ______ (not speak) one language. They ______ (speak) three languages.
3 They ______ (not talk) about rules now. They ______ (talk) about problems.
4 He usually ______ (work) alone. He ______ (not work) with a friend.
5 The teacher ______ (not give) us homework on Mondays. But she ______ (give) us a lot of homework on Fridays!
6 Sam is in her room at the moment. She ______ (listen) to some music and she ______ (play) a computer game.

6 **Read the video script. Underline any words or phrases you don't know and find their meaning in your dictionary.**

Byron Court School

Many schools have students of different nationalities. In the playground at one school in London you can hear not five languages, not fifteen, not thirty, but forty-two! Byron Court is a primary school with 600 children from five to eleven years old. They are from Somalia, Iraq, Poland, Romania, Nepal, the Philippines and many more. And, oh yes, of course, from England! This part of London has families from all over the world. They come to live and work in London.

Many children don't speak English when they start. It can be a problem. But with good teachers and friends they learn fast. Soon their English is good and their school work is good too. The children at this school get to know children from different countries. They're laughing and talking together. It's great for them to have friends from different countries.

At Byron Court the children don't only do school work. They learn about different cultures. They also learn to work together. A good example for everyone.

5 The music of life

VOCABULARY
Musical instruments | Types of music

GRAMMAR
Comparatives | Superlatives

READING
A music video show

LISTENING
Live music

SPEAKING
Making suggestions

WRITING
Texts and tweets

BBC CULTURE
Why do we play musical instruments?

5.1 VOCABULARY Music

I can talk about types of music and musical instruments.

1 ● **Look at the photos and complete the word puzzle. What's the hidden word?**

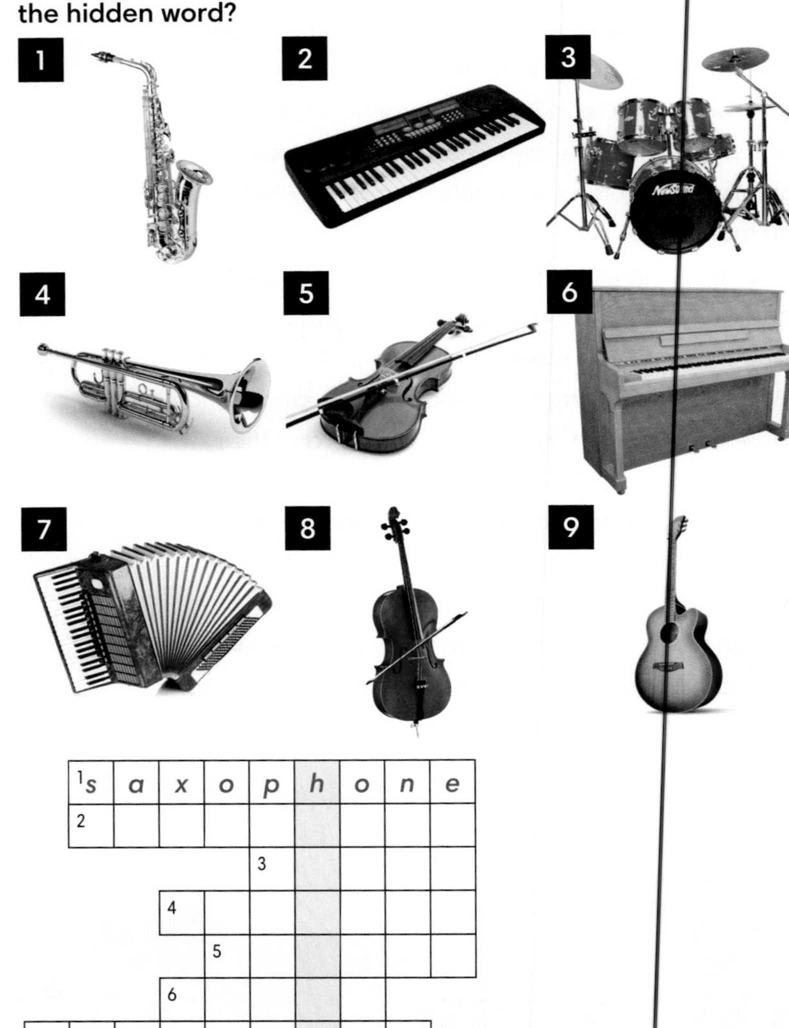

	1 *s*	*a*	*x*	*o*	*p*	*h*	*o*	*n*	*e*	
	2									
					3					
			4							
				5						
			6							
7										
						8				
		9								

The hidden word is: ________________ .

2 ●● **Choose the correct option.**

1 My brother has got some (*drums*) / *keyboards* but he plays them in the garage because they're very loud!
2 I've got a *guitar* / *harmonica*. It's great because I can carry it in my pocket.
3 I've got a *flute* / *cello*. I can carry it but it's very big and very heavy!
4 I like playing the *accordion* / *drums* but you need strong arms to push it in and out.
5 The *trumpet* / *piano* is a lovely instrument but it's expensive and you can't carry it.
6 My sister is trying to learn the *piano* / *violin*. It's really difficult and the noise is like a cat!

3 ● Match pictures A–H with words 1–8.

A

B

C

D

E

F

G

H

1 [F] traditional
2 [ ] country
3 [ ] classical
4 [ ] pop
5 [ ] reggae
6 [ ] jazz
7 [ ] techno
8 [ ] hip-hop

4 ● Find eight types of music in the word search. Look ↑, ↓, ↗ and ↘.

A	Y	N	Z	J	A	E	R	J	M	N
Q	T	F	A	J	C	W	G	C	F	W
N	O	E	U	O	A	T	V	E	A	Y
D	H	S	W	W	F	Z	I	E	R	T
S	R	I	P	Z	W	G	Z	T	E	P
X	A	O	P	X	T	E	N	E	G	V
S	P	D	S	H	H	U	B	C	G	D
T	O	M	N	P	O	I	O	H	A	P
A	F	R	O	C	K	P	N	N	E	V
R	A	K	V	R	E	L	S	O	R	K
M	Y	X	E	E	T	E	M	N	R	M

5 ●● Order the letters and write the words in the sentences.

1 My brother's got a lot of *rock* (cokr) music. It's very loud and he plays it on his guitar too.

2 __________ (hotcen) music is a type of electronic music and it often repeats the same bits again and again.

3 I like __________ (laslacics) music because it's soft and I can relax.

4 There's a dance to __________ (ctroynu) music. You stand in a long line and do the same moves.

5 I think __________ (ergage) music comes from countries like Jamaica.

6 My sister loves __________ (riattanolid) Irish music with accordions and guitars.

6 ●●● Complete the words in the dialogue.

Liz: Do you play any [1]**i***n s t r u m e n t s*?

Jim: Yes I play the [2]**g**_ _ _ _ _ in a band.

Liz: Really? What sort of [3]**g**_ _ _ _ _ ?

Jim: It's a [4]**b**_ _ _ . It's great fun. Our band is very loud!

Liz: What [5]**k**_ _ _ of music do you play?

Jim: We play [6]**r**_ _ _ . Do you like [7]**r**_ _ _ music?

Liz: It's OK but I prefer [8]**c**_ _ _ _ _ _ _ _ or [9]**j**_ _ _ . I play the [10]**v**_ _ _ _ _ and the [11]**s**_ _ _ _ _ _ _ _ . How many people are in your band?

Jim: There are three of us, but we're looking for more people. We can't play the [12]**d**_ _ _ _ or the [13]**k**_ _ _ _ _ _ _ .

Liz: My brother plays the [14]**k**_ _ _ _ _ _ _ .

Jim: Great! Ask him to call me!

5.2 GRAMMAR Comparatives

I can make comparisons.

1 ● **Write the comparative form of the adjectives below in the correct column.**

big ~~cheap~~ cute dark difficult easy excited expensive friendly funny nice pretty slim successful thin

brave**r**/ rich**er**	sad**der**	happ**ier**	**more** interesting
cheaper			

2 ●● **Write two comparative sentences about each picture.**

1 tall / short
Tim is taller than Max.
Max is shorter than Tim.

2 rich / poor
______
______

3 long / short
______
______

4 young / old
______
______

5 expensive / cheap
______
______

6 easy / difficult
______
______

3 ●● **Write comparative sentences about Anna and Brian. Use *better* or *worse*.**

	Anna	Brian
1 violin player	☺	☺☺
2 cook	☹☹	☹
3 artist	☺☺	☺
4 student	☺	☺☺
5 driver	☺☺	☺
6 dancer	☹	☹☹
7 singer	☹☹	☹
8 swimmer	☺	☺☺

1 *Brian is a better violin player than Anna.*
2 *Anna is a worse cook than Brian.*
3 ______
4 ______
5 ______
6 ______
7 ______
8 ______

4 ●●● **Complete the text with the comparative form of the adjectives below.**

bad ~~busy~~ expensive fast friendly funny high intelligent tall thin

My best friend Jade and I are the same age but we're very different! Jade has lots of hobbies and her life is [1]*busier* than mine. She's also [2]______ – six centimetres – and [3]______ – three kilos. I think she's [4]______ than me because her grades are always [5]______ than mine! I'm good at tennis and I always win – she's a [6]______ player than I am but she's a [7]______ swimmer. I wear [8]______ clothes than Jade does and my jokes are [9]______ than hers! We've both got dogs. Her dog, Josh, is definitely [10]______ than my dog, Chubby. Josh is very scared of Chubby!

5.7 WRITING Texts and tweets

I can write short messages (texts or tweets).

1 Read the messages. Which words can you leave out? The number is in brackets.

1 ~~I~~ love ~~the~~ new album. (2)

2 I'm back home. I'll ring you in 15 minutes! (2)

3 I'm going swimming later. Do you want to come? (3)

4 This homework is terrible. I can't do it! (3)

5 The new film is fantastic! (2)

2 Match symbols and abbreviations 1–8 with words a–h.

1 [c] @ 3 [ ] 4 5 [ ] C 7 [ ] R
2 [ ] 2 4 [ ] B 6 [ ] U 8 [ ] Y

a why c at e to g for
b are d see f be h you

3 Match the abbreviations with their meanings below.

~~bye for now~~ great later laughing out loud please thanks tomorrow tonight wait

1 bfn *bye for now*
2 lol ______
3 gr8 ______
4 w8 ______
5 l8r ______
6 thx ______
7 plz ______
8 2nite ______
9 2moro ______

4 What do the emojis mean? Complete the words/phrases.

1 ☹ I'm s*ad*.
2 ☺ I'm **h**______.
3 😮 I'm **s**______.
4 ♥ I **l**______ it!
5 😘 **K**______!

5 Write out the texts with all the words.

1 Cu 2moro @ concert. Can't w8!

See you tomorrow at the concert. I can't wait!

2 R u OK? Come round l8r. Bfn

______

3 Got test results 2day. Gr8. So ☺

______

4 Y r u not @ school? Call me.😘

______

5 Gr8 present! ♥ Thx.

______

6 Can u get ticket 4 me 4 concert plz?

______

6 Make the text shorter. Use symbols, abbreviations and emojis from this page.

Great to see you today. Thanks for your help with my homework! I'm happy! Can you come to my party at Benny's café tomorrow? See you there! Love and kisses.

Gr8 ______

7 Write a text to a friend and his/her reply. Use symbols, abbreviations and emojis from this page. Remember to do these things.

In your text:

- give some good, bad or surprising news.
- make a suggestion.
- arrange a time to meet.

In the reply:

- respond to the news.
- respond to the suggestion.
- agree with or suggest another time.

5.8 SELF-ASSESSMENT

For each learning objective, tick (✓) the box that best matches your ability.

☺☺ = I understand and can help a friend.

☺ = I understand and can do it by myself.

☹ = I understand but have some questions.

☹☹ = I do not understand.

		☺☺	☺	☹	☹☹	Need help?	Now try ...
5.1	Vocabulary					Students' Book pp. 58–59 Workbook pp. 54–55	Ex. 1–3, p. 63
5.2	Grammar					Students' Book p. 60 Workbook p. 56	Ex. 4, p. 63
5.3	Reading					Students' Book p. 61 Workbook p. 57	
5.4	Grammar					Students' Book p. 62 Workbook p. 58	Ex. 5, p. 63
5.5	Listening					Students' Book p. 63 Workbook p. 59	
5.6	Speaking					Students' Book p. 64 Workbook p. 60	Ex. 6, p. 63
5.7	Writing					Students' Book p. 65 Workbook p. 61	

5.1 I can talk about types of music and musical instruments.
5.2 I can make comparisons.
5.3 I can find specific detail in reviews and give opinions about music programmes.
5.4 I can use superlatives to compare more than two people or things.
5.5 I can identify specific detail in a radio programme and talk about live music.
5.6 I can make and respond to suggestions.
5.7 I can write short messages (texts or tweets).

What can you remember from this unit?

New words I learned (the words you most want to remember from this unit)	**Expressions and phrases I liked** (any expressions or phrases you think sound nice, useful or funny)	**English I heard or read outside class** (e.g. from websites, books, adverts, films, music)

Vocabulary

1 Look at the photos and write the musical instruments.

1 ______________

2 ______________

3 ______________

4 ______________

5 ______________

6 ______________

7 ______________

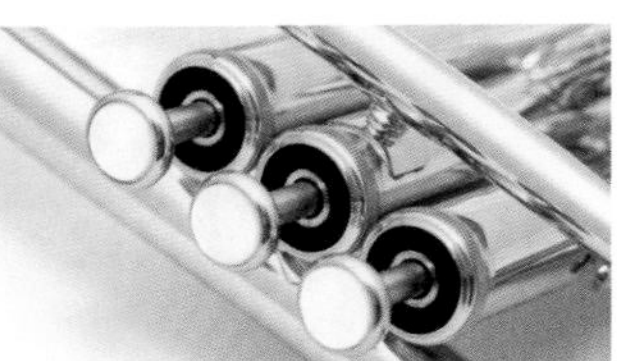

8 ______________

2 Complete the words in the review.

Don't miss the new film *Charlie*. It's [1]**f**_ _ _ _ _ _ _ _! It's got some very funny jokes, the actors are [2]**b**_ _ _ _ _ _ _ _ and the directing is [3]**g**_ _ _ _. There's another new film on at the moment, *Cry of the Dark*, but don't go! Everything about it is [4]**t**_ _ _ _ _ _ _ – the acting, the story, the photography ... It's a very [5]**b**_ _ _ _ film. *Night in Cape Cod* is a little better. The photography is [6]**c**_ _ _ and the story is [7]**a**_ _ _ _ _ _. But if you can only see one film, it's got to be *Charlie*!

3 Complete the words.

1 This is a group of people who sing and play music: **b**_ _ _
2 These people watch a concert: **a**_ _ _ _ _ _ _
3 Singers and actors go on this to perform: **s**_ _ _ _
4 This person plays an instrument: **m**_ _ _ _ _ _ _
5 This is a type of music: **r**_ _ _

Grammar

4 Complete the sentences with the comparative form of the adjectives below.

bad cheap difficult excited good happy

1 My grades are ________ than my best friend's. I'm a good student!
2 Let's go by bus. It's ________ than the train.
3 Jimmy is ________ than his sister about the party.
4 It's ________ to learn the violin than the guitar.
5 This song is ________ than the group's last song. I don't like it.
6 In this photo you are ________ than in that one.

5 Choose the correct answer.

1 *Rain* is ___ song on the album.
   a worse than b the worst
2 Is David the ___ person in your family? His room is always really untidy!
   a lazier than b laziest
3 Jane is ___ I am! She always gets top marks in tests.
   a more intelligent than
   b the most intelligent
4 The ___ person in my class is Rowan.
   a fitter b fittest
5 The Jacksons' restaurant is ___ Benny's. It's always full of people.
   a more popular than
   b the most popular
6 Matt Johnson is ___ actor on TV. I always laugh at his jokes and stories.
   a funnier b the funniest

Speaking language practice

6 Complete the sentences with one or two words in each gap.

1 ________ do you suggest?
2 ________ you got any other suggestions?
3 ________ I make a suggestion?
4 ________ not?
5 ________ not a good idea.
6 ________ go to the new shopping centre.
7 ________ don't you have a break?
8 ________ about a cup of tea?

1 Find the words below in the word search. Look ↑, ↓, ↗ and ↘.

~~brain~~ hearing intelligence physical rewarding scientist team

S	R	E	W	A	R	D	I	N	G
O	Y	T	(B)	F	O	Z	N	U	S
I	H	T	(R)	W	V	R	T	D	C
D	T	K	(A)	H	B	T	E	E	I
P	P	O	(I)	E	E	E	L	P	E
D	J	N	(N)	A	Y	A	L	K	N
B	U	A	F	R	C	M	I	V	T
W	Z	D	J	I	V	U	G	D	I
S	F	Q	S	N	T	V	E	D	S
M	V	Y	X	G	Z	N	N	H	T
P	H	R	F	B	A	U	C	C	I
P	S	S	Z	L	D	N	E	B	T
Q	N	K	Q	O	Q	C	I	T	I

2 Complete the sentences with words from Exercise 1.

1. Speak louder. Gran's *hearing* isn't very good!
2. Running and swimming are ________ activities.
3. Vitamins are good for your body and your ________ . They can help your memory.
4. Paul wants to be a ________ when he's older.
5. When people like my music, I feel good. It's very ________ .
6. This ________ test is very difficult. I can't do it.
7. At school we often work in a ________ .

3 Choose the correct option.

1. Playing music gives you a great *feel* / (*feeling*).
2. It's good to play music *at* / *with* other people.
3. Music is good *at* / *for* us in many ways.
4. Children *aged* / *ages* five can start school.
5. Listening to music can help *on* / *with* a lot of problems.

4 Complete the sentences with the words below.

audition copy download ~~join~~ make practise

1. Lots of young people want to *join* an orchestra.
2. Every evening I go online and I ________ information for my homework.
3. Watch the teacher and ________ what she does.
4. I ________ the guitar every day. I'm getting better.
5. Let's ________ a video and put it online.
6. I want to ________ for the school show.

5 Match photos A–E with sentences 1–5.

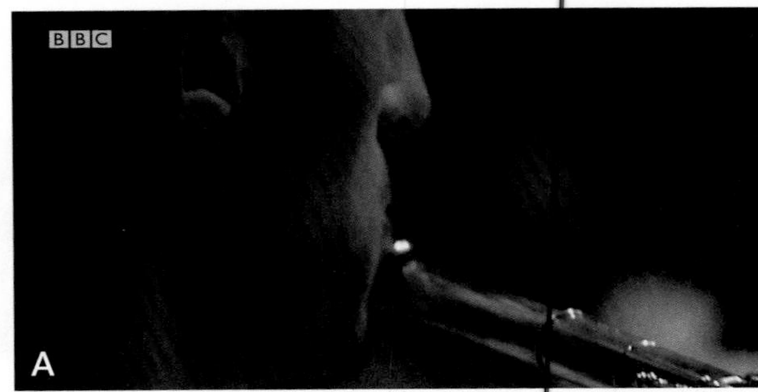
A

B

C

D

E

1. ☐ They're playing music and dancing.
2. ☐ She's playing the cello.
3. ☐ He's playing the double bass.
4. ☐ He's playing the flute.
5. ☐ They're playing instruments together.

6 **Read the video script. Underline any words or phrases you don't know and find their meaning in your dictionary.**

National Youth Orchestra of Iraq

Tu'qa plays the cello in an orchestra. Together with other young musicians, she's in Scotland to play some concerts. Teenagers in an orchestra – is that unusual? No. But for these teenagers it is unusual. In their country they can't practise together. It's too dangerous. These teenagers haven't got teachers. They are all self-taught. They download music from the internet. They watch people with instruments online and they copy them. Then they practise and practise. Zuhal is seventeen and the orchestra is her idea. She wants the young people in her country to play together. To join the orchestra, the players make a video and put it online. Tu'qa is auditioning through YouTube. This is Waleed Ahmed Assi. He plays the flute. He's brilliant. This is Chia Sultan. He plays the double bass. He learns from YouTube and practises in his room. Now the teenagers are having a break from practice. It's time for a party. They're playing music and dancing. They love it. Here in Scotland they are having a wonderful time. They love music. And playing music together is easier now. They want to come again.

6

A question of sport

VOCABULARY
Sports | Sportspeople | Collocations: *score a goal*, *win a match*, etc. | Sports competitions | Interests and hobbies: collocations with *go*, *do* and *play*

GRAMMAR
was/were | *there was/there were* | Past Simple affirmative (regular and irregular verbs)

READING
Places to play sport

LISTENING
Sporting moments

SPEAKING
Hobbies and interests

ENGLISH IN USE
ago

BBC CULTURE
When did football begin?

EXAM TIME 2 > p. 118

VOCABULARY Sports

I can talk about sports and sportspeople.

1 ● **Match pictures A–J with words 1–10.**

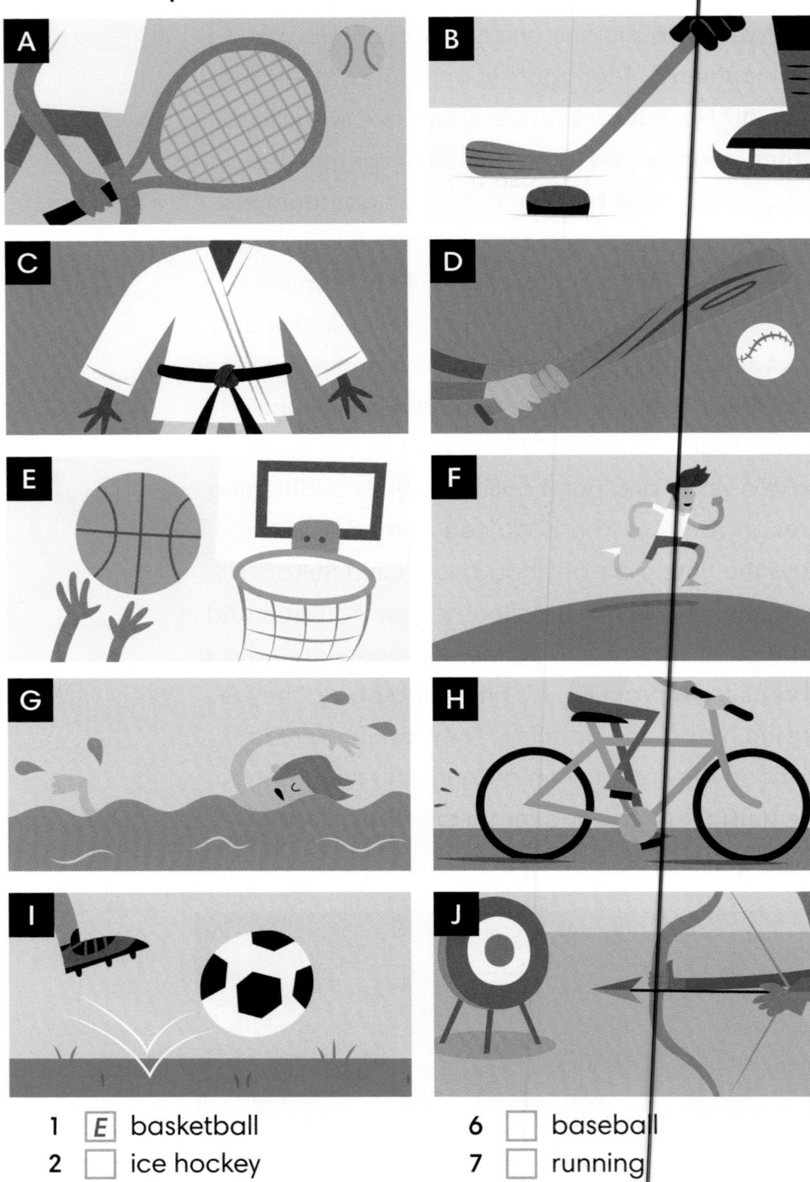

1 [E] basketball
2 [ ] ice hockey
3 [ ] football
4 [ ] archery
5 [ ] judo
6 [ ] baseball
7 [ ] running
8 [ ] tennis
9 [ ] swimming
10 [ ] cycling

2 ●● **Read the descriptions and write the sports.**

1 You stand a long way from a circle and try to hit it. *archery*
2 You can do this in the sea or in a pool. ______
3 You skate and push something around with a stick. ______
4 You wear a white jacket and trousers and different coloured belts. ______
5 People who are very tall are good at this because you need to jump high. ______
6 You do this sport in the town or the country and wear a special hat. ______

3 ● What do we call the people who do these sports?

1 football *a player*
2 running ________
3 cycling ________
4 tennis ________
5 ice hockey ________
6 basketball ________
7 swimming ________
8 baseball ________

4 ● WORD FRIENDS Choose the correct option.

1 *win* / *score* / *play* a goal
2 *win* / *score* / *play* a sport
3 *win* / *score* / *play* a race
4 *win* / *score* / *play* a medal
5 *win* / *score* / *play* a point

5 ●● WORD FRIENDS Choose the correct option.

1 How many sports do you *score* / *play*?
2 Tom usually plays a football *point* / *match* on Saturdays.
3 I love this photo. It's the 100 metres and Tom is *scoring* / *winning* his race.
4 The USA always *play* / *win* a lot of medals at the Olympic Games.
5 This is a really strange sport! How do you score a *race* / *point*?
6 Bale regularly *plays* / *scores* goals for his football team.
7 We hope to *win* / *score* lots of matches this year and go into the national competition.

6 ●● Complete the crossword.

Across

3 A ________ rides a bike.
5 We need one more ________ to win the table tennis game.
7 Baseball isn't an ________ sport.
10 On Saturday there's a football ________ between our school and yours.
13 In ________, you stand very still and use your arms.
14 You need special shoes for ________ on roads.
15 ________ is frozen water and people can do sports on it.

Down

1 We can ________ the match today! I'm sure!
2 When there's a ________ in a football match, everyone shouts!
4 I love ________ in the sea but we don't live near the seaside.
6 Ice ________ is a popular sport in cold countries.
8 The ________ is only ten seconds – you must run very fast!
9 In judo, you ________ a point when you throw your opponent to the floor.
11 There are eleven players in a football ________.
12 Wimbledon is a very famous ________ competition.

7 ●●● Complete the dialogue with one word in each gap.

Angie: Do you still [1]*play* football?

Brian: Yes, I'm in the school [2]________. We have a [3]________ every week.

Angie: Great! Do you usually [4]________?

Brian: Yes, we're good! But I don't usually [5]________ goals because my job is to stop the other team! Why don't you come to practice? You can play too.

Angie: No, thanks. I prefer [6]________ sports because I can choose my time to practise. And I'm not very good at playing with other people! I love [7]________, but at the moment my bike's broken.

Brian: So, you're a [8]________. Do you do competitions?

Angie: Sometimes. There's a [9]________ across the hills and through the town every summer. I do that. It's fun – and I usually win!

6.2 GRAMMAR *was/were*

I can use *was/were* to talk about events in the past.

1 ● Choose the correct option.

1 I (*was*) / *were* born in 2000.
2 You *was* / *were* in Canada in 2015.
3 Tim *was* / *were* in a hockey team last year.
4 The film *was* / *were* very boring.
5 We *was* / *were* tired.
6 The basketball players *was* / *were* tall and fast.
7 My mum *was* / *were* very good at sports.

2 ● Complete the sentences with *was* or *were*.

1 Jack *was* the best player in the team last month.
2 My friends, Susie and Mike, _______ in London last weekend.
3 1D's music _______ popular last year.
4 I know you! You _______ at Luke's party on Friday.
5 Katy and I were in the park today and Izzy _______ there with her boyfriend.
6 Bruno's café _______ the cheapest café in town last year but it isn't now.
7 Our teacher _______ in the classroom before us today.
8 I _______ at home all day yesterday.

3 ●● Correct the sentences. Make the underlined parts negative.

1 I was at school yesterday because I was at the dentist's.
I wasn't at school
2 There was any milk in the fridge this morning, so no breakfast!
____
3 There were many people at the match yesterday and it was very quiet.
____
4 My answers were correct and the teacher was happy! She was very angry.
____
5 Jim's birthday party was on Saturday. It was on Friday.
____
6 Last time the coffee here was very good and the biscuits were dry. Let's try something else.
____
7 The football players were very fit and the result was very good. In fact, it was terrible!
____
8 My brother and I were at home yesterday morning. We were at the sports centre.
____

4 ●● Order the words to make questions.

1 match / the / Friday / football / was / exciting / on / ?
Was the football match on Friday exciting?
2 you / where / yesterday / were / ?
____
3 your / Year 9 / teacher / was / in / who / ?
____
4 you / team / were / in / last / year / the / ?
____
5 dad / was / good / student / a / your / ?
____
6 was / favourite / which / year / film / last / your / ?
____

5 ●●● Complete the email with the correct form of *was* or *were*.

To: david@fastmessage.com

Hi David,

Our holiday [1]*was* fantastic. We [2]_______ in a small town in Spain and the sea [3]_______ very near. Our hotel [4]_______ very big – only ten rooms – so there [5]_______ crowds of people at meal times and the beach [6]_______ nice and quiet. The weather [7]_______ lovely and very hot! I [8]_______ in the water a lot of the time. But some of the staff [9]_______ very friendly and they [10]_______ always too busy to answer our questions.

How about you? How [11]_______ your exams? [12]_______ you pleased with the results? And [13]_______ there lots of people at your birthday party? I'm sorry I [14]_______ there!

See you soon,
Lara

6.3 READING and VOCABULARY A young sports star

I can find specific detail in a text and talk about places to play sport.

1 **Look at the photos and complete the words.**

1 basketball **c**o u r t

2 football **f**_ _ _ _ / football **p**_ _ _ _

3 tennis **c**_ _ _ _

4 swimming **p**_ _ _

5 running **t**_ _ _ _

2 **Complete the sentences with words from Exercise 1.**

1 We can't play football today because the *field* is too wet!
2 I really want to play basketball but the __________ is closed.
3 I'm at the leisure centre but the __________ is full. I don't like swimming when there are too many people.
4 Come to the __________ after school and we can do some running training.
5 Andy is playing tennis on __________ number 2. We can watch him.

3 **Read the text and complete the information below.**

Perfect!

Gymnastics is a very popular sport. Millions of people watch it on TV and lots of children do gymnastics at school and in clubs. One of the most famous gymnasts ever is a young gymnast from Romania: Nadia Comaneci.

Nadia is Romanian and she was born in 1961. Today Nadia is a wife and mother but when she was only fourteen years old, she was the best gymnast in the world. At the Summer Olympic Games in Montreal, Canada in 1976, she was really amazing. She was the first Romanian gymnast to win the all-round title, for all the different gymnastic events. She was also the youngest in the world. Now the age rules are different and gymnasts can't compete under the age of sixteen. So the record is Nadia's for ever!

She was also amazing in 1976 for another reason. She was the first gymnast to score a perfect 10.00. It was her first event, the uneven bars. On the scoreboard after her thirty-second routine, the score was 1.00. Everyone was confused. Why was it only 1.00? She was fantastic! It was because the scoreboard only had three numbers. For example, 9.75 was possible, but not 10.00! After this, at the same Olympics, Nadia's score was 10.00 for six more events. She was a real star. Perfect Nadia!

Name: [1] *Nadia Comaneci*
Nationality: [2] __________
Year she was born: [3] __________
Year, country, town of Summer Olympics: [4] __________, [5] __________, [6] __________
First event: [7] __________
Score on scoreboard: [8] __________
Real score: [9] __________
Number of perfect scores: [10] __________

4 **Read the text again. Mark the sentences ✓ (right), ✗ (wrong) or ? (doesn't say).**

1 ☐ Nadia is married today.
2 ☐ She was sixteen at the Montreal Olympics.
3 ☐ In 1976 the age limit for gymnasts was lower than today.
4 ☐ Her first routine was one minute long.
5 ☐ The scoreboard was wrong because it was broken.
6 ☐ Nadia has gold medals from two Olympic Games.

Past Simple affirmative (regular and irregular verbs)

I can use the Past Simple to talk about events in the past.

1 **Complete the sentences with the words below.**

OUT of class

on poor ~~shot~~ wrong

1 Good *shot* ! You scored a goal!
2 I want to go to the concert. When's it ________ ?
3 A: I can't come out. I've got lots of homework.
B: ________ you!
4 A: What's ________ ?
B: We lost the match.

2 ● **Look at the pictures and complete the sentences. Use the Past Simple form of the verbs below.**

~~call~~ email jog kiss paint play

1 He *called* me at 11.30 last night.

2 We ________ along the road this morning.

3 They ________ cards after dinner.

4 She ________ me on the train.

5 I ________ my baby sister before school.

6 Erin ________ a picture of flowers at school.

3 ●● **Find and correct the mistakes in the sentences. Two sentences are correct.**

1 Paul runned a marathon last weekend.
Paul ran a marathon last weekend.
2 I tryed to make an omelette but it was terrible.
____
3 In class yesterday we made a poster for the school play.
____
4 Janine walkd to school this morning.
____
5 We went to the park after school and I taked some photographs on my phone.
____
6 Katy founded an old exercise book from Year 5.
____
7 I know I put the biscuits on this shelf. Where are they?
____

4 ●●● **Complete the blog with the Past Simple form of the verbs below.**

cook do eat ~~get up~~ go have listen play relax see take watch

myblog

What an excellent weekend! On Saturday morning I [1] *got up* very late because I was so tired. Then, after breakfast – my favourite full English – Tony and I [2] ________ to the leisure centre. It's amazing! There's a big pool and lots of courts. We [3] ________ tennis and then we [4] ________ a volleyball match for half an hour. The players were very fast and very good. Too energetic for me! And in the evening Tony [5] ________ me to the cinema and we [6] ________ the new Jennifer Lawrence film. It was brilliant! On Sunday I [7] ________ in the morning and then, in the afternoon, Mum and Dad [8] ________ a barbecue in the garden. They [9] ________ sausages and burgers. They were delicious and I [10] ________ too many! On Sunday evening I [11] ________ some homework (ugh!) and [12] ________ to some music.

How was your weekend?

I can identify specific detail in a radio sports programme and talk about a sports match.

1 Complete the words in the sentences.

1 My friend is playing in a big tennis **t**o u r n a m e n t at the moment. It happens every year.
2 My dad's really happy. His favourite football team won their match yesterday and now they're in the top **l**_ _ _ _ _.
3 Don't get excited! You won the **s**_ _ _-**f**_ _ _ _ but now you're playing Serena in the **f**_ _ _ _. And she's very good!
4 My mum was a good swimmer and she's got a big **c**_ _ on the shelf in her room. She won it in a national competition when she was fifteen.

2 WORD FRIENDS Choose the correct option.

1 I hope we don't *win* / *lose* this match. The winner gets a lovely cup.
2 Let's *get* / *go* cycling this afternoon. It's lovely and sunny.
3 Which team does Bale play *at* / *for*?
4 Let's *do* / *play* badminton later.
5 My brother *did* / *played* judo when he was younger. He was quite good.
6 It's important to *make* / *do* some exercise every day to keep fit.

3 15 Listen to four phone conversations (1–4). Match them with sentences a–d.

a ☐ The girl talks about a new sport she started.
b ☐ The boy and girl talk about a regular activity.
c ☐ The boy and girl plan to do something together.
d ☐ The boy talks about something he did on holiday.

4 15 Listen again. Choose the correct answer.

1 What do the boy and girl plan to do together?

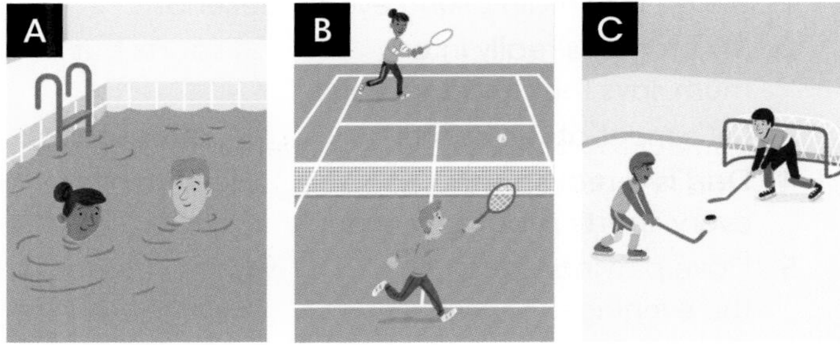

2 What day was the Yankees game?

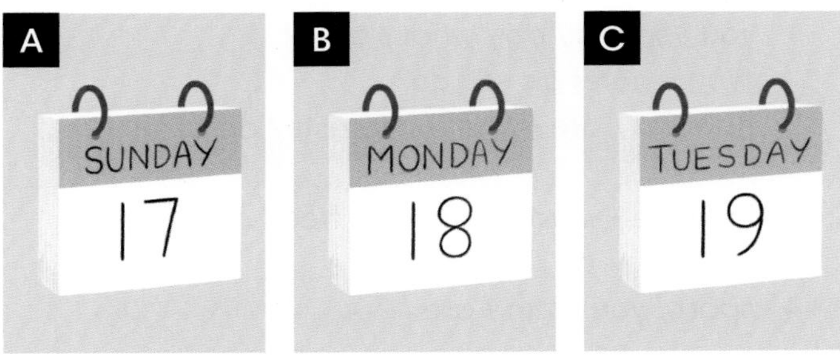

3 How long does the girl usually jog each morning?

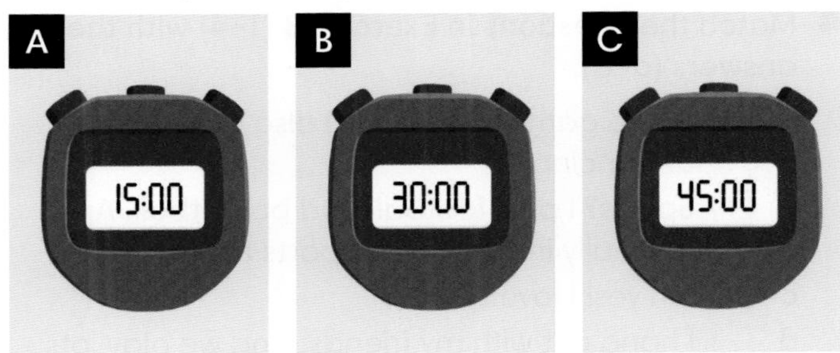

4 How much do clothes cost for the girl's new sport?

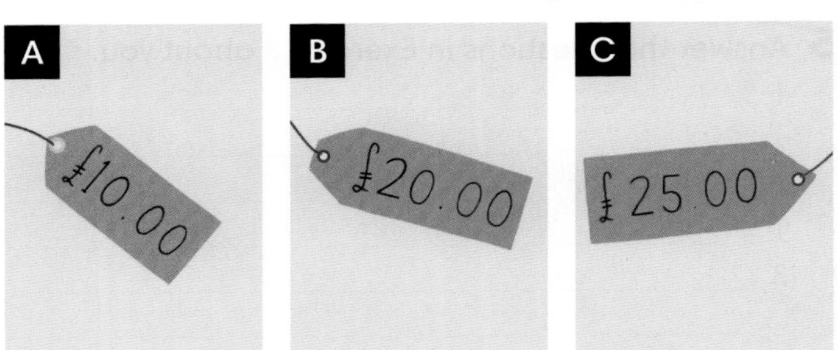

Talking about hobbies and interests

I can talk about hobbies and interests.

1 Complete the response with one word. OUT of class

A: Which is your favourite sport?
B: To be ________ , I don't like sports much. I prefer books and films.

2 Complete the sentences with the words below.

~~biking~~ centre extreme fanatic games

1 We go mountain *biking* every weekend.
2 My brother's really into ________ sports but mum says they're dangerous.
3 Let's meet at the sports ________ after school.
4 Dad is a real sports ________ . He watches every sports programme on TV!
5 I love playing video ________ with my friends in the evenings.

3 Order the words to make questions.

1 you / sports / do / what / do / ?
What sports do you do?
2 hobbies / are / what / interests / and / your / ?
____
3 in / time / what / you / do / free / do / your / ?
____
4 sport / you / into / are / ?
____

4 Match the questions in Exercise 3 (1–4) with these answers (a–d).

a ☐ Video games and judo! I also do a lot of dancing.
b ☐ *1* Sports? I play football and basketball. And I'm really into extreme sports too.
c ☐ Oh yes! I love sport!
d ☐ I hang out with my friends. And we play lots and lots of video games!

5 Answer the questions in Exercise 3 about you.

1 ________
2 ________
3 ________
4 ________

6 Choose the correct answer.

1 I ___ running.
a play (b) go c do
2 I hang ___ with my friends.
a on b at c out
3 I'm interested ___ extreme sports.
a in b on c at
4 I'm really ___ water sports.
a in for b into c on at
5 I'm not very keen ___ sport.
a at b up c on
6 I ___ a lot of judo.
a do b play c go
7 I'm a big fan ___ skateboarding.
a to b of c along
8 I ___ video games.
a do b play c go
9 So, what do you do ___ your free time?
a for b in c on
10 I also ___ a lot of dancing.
a play b go c do

7 Complete the dialogue with sentences a–f.

Ben: Hi! Where is everyone?
Kim: [1] *e*
Ben: And you aren't?
Kim: [2] ___
Ben: How about football? There's a match on later.
Kim: [3] ___
Ben: OK. So, what do you do in your free time?
Kim: [4] ___
Ben: Yeah, I'm interested in music too.
Kim: [5] ___
Ben: Yes, I am. I do a lot of judo. But they never show that on TV.
Kim: Right.
Ben: [6] ___

a No, I'm not really into sport – especially football!
b No, I'm doing some homework. I'm not very keen on tennis.
c But I'm a bit bored, so maybe tennis on the TV is a good idea. Enjoy your homework!
d And are you into sport?
e Oh they're watching the tennis on TV.
f Well, I love dancing and listening to music.

6.7 ENGLISH IN USE *ago*

I can use *ago* to talk about events in the past.

1 Put *ago* or *at* in the correct place in the sentences. Some sentences need both words.

1 I got up ten minutes.
I got up ten minutes ago.
2 Three years I went to the USA with my parents.
______
3 We started our lesson 9.30 and we finished half an hour.
______
4 My friend arrived in England a week and she leaves tonight nine o'clock.
______
5 It started to rain an hour and we've got a football match 3.15!
______

2 Order the words to make sentences.

1 I / new / months / school / two / started / ago / a
I started a new school two months ago.
2 years / to / we / this / town / moved / five / ago
______
3 the / ago / two / started / minutes / film
______
4 I / the / ago / to / match / three / football / went / days
______
5 built / the / ago / Romans / Colosseum / centuries / the
______

3 Look at the pictures and complete the sentences. Use *ago*.

From: Mark Stephens
Subject: Ella's birthday party
Date: 12 February
Received: 4.30 p.m.
4.30

1 It's 6.30. The email arrived *two hours ago*.

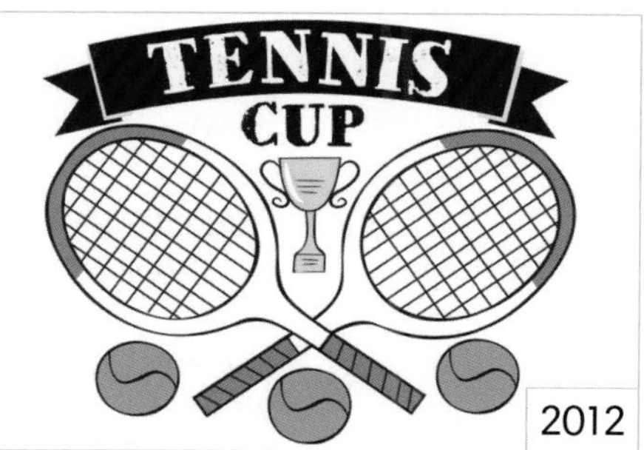

2 Our school's first tennis tournament took place ______.

3 It's 3.25. The race started ______.

4 It's 2.15. Wendy won the cup ______.

5 It's Thursday. Sally arrived in Spain ______.

6 It's May. Dad bought his car ______.

4 Complete the blog with one word in each gap.

There's a sports centre near our home with a big swimming [1] *pool* and some badminton [2] ______. I started to [3] ______ badminton six months [4] ______ and now I go every week. My brother isn't very [5] ______ on sports but he likes watching sport on TV. He's a [6] ______ of Southampton football club and sometimes goes to their [7] ______. They got into the [8] ______ of the Football League Cup two months [9] ______ and he watched it live in London. They [10] ______, but he enjoyed the match! I'm not really [11] ______ football but I like it when Southampton [12] ______.

6.8 SELF-ASSESSMENT

For each learning objective, tick (✓) the box that best matches your ability.

☺☺ = I understand and can help a friend.

☺ = I understand and can do it by myself.

☹ = I understand but have some questions.

☹☹ = I do not understand.

		☺☺	☺	☹	☹☹	Need help?	Now try ...
6.1	Vocabulary					Students' Book pp. 70–71 Workbook pp. 66–67	Ex. 1–3, p. 75
6.2	Grammar					Students' Book p. 72 Workbook p. 68	Ex. 4, p. 75
6.3	Reading					Students' Book p. 73 Workbook p. 69	
6.4	Grammar					Students' Book p. 74 Workbook p. 70	Ex. 5, p. 75
6.5	Listening					Students' Book p. 75 Workbook p. 71	
6.6	Speaking					Students' Book p. 76 Workbook p. 72	Ex. 7, p. 75
6.7	English in use					Students' Book p. 77 Workbook p. 73	Ex. 6, p. 75

6.1 I can talk about sports and sportspeople.
6.2 I can use *was/were* to talk about events in the past.
6.3 I can find specific detail in a text and talk about places to play sport.
6.4 I can use the Past Simple to talk about events in the past.
6.5 I can identify specific detail in a radio sports programme and talk about a sports match.
6.6 I can talk about hobbies and interests.
6.7 I can use *ago* to talk about events in the past.

What can you remember from this unit?

New words I learned (the words you most want to remember from this unit)	**Expressions and phrases I liked** (any expressions or phrases you think sound nice, useful or funny)	**English I heard or read outside class** (e.g. from websites, books, adverts, films, music)

6.9 SELF-CHECK

Vocabulary

1 Choose the correct option.

1 *Tennis* / *Football* is a racket sport.
2 *Baseball* / *Archery* is an individual sport.
3 *Ice hockey* / *Running* is a team sport.
4 *Judo* / *Basketball* is a ball game.

2 Complete the sentences with the words below.

cup cyclist medals pitch points score team

1 Our national football team always takes part in the World ________ .
2 A: What was the ________ ?
B: 2–2.
3 How many ________ do you need to win a table tennis game?
4 I'm angry because I'm not in the school basketball ________ . I'm too short!
5 Sometimes spectators come onto the ________ at the end of the match.
6 Chris Hoy is a famous ________ who won lots of gold ________ at the Olympic Games.

3 Choose the correct option.

1 The tennis *courts* / *pitches* were all busy, so we went swimming.
2 Do you *do* / *go* jogging every morning?
3 I haven't got my trainers. I think they're still by the *swimming* / *running* track.
4 Andy played in the semi-final but unfortunately, he *lost* / *failed* the match.
5 My sister really wants to *go* / *do* judo but my dad doesn't think it's a good idea.
6 At school we run round the football *field* / *court* at the beginning of every sports lesson.

Grammar

4 Complete the sentences with the correct form of *was* or *were*.

1 Jim ________ the worst runner in my class at primary school. He always lost races.
2 We ________ at home at the weekend. We went to the seaside.
3 ________ you at Donna's party on Friday?
4 Who ________ your first teacher?
5 ________ the weather good when you ________ on holiday last week?
6 I ________ interested in sports when I ________ young. But I am now.

5 Complete the sentences with the Past Simple form of the verbs below.

end go play run score see shout wait watch win

1 I was in town yesterday and I ________ Lyn with her new boyfriend.
2 We ________ the match on TV and everyone ________ when Rooney ________ a goal!
3 We ________ for a walk after lunch.
4 At sports day Bill ________ faster than everyone and he ________ the race.
5 The teacher ________ us some English songs in class. They were cool.
6 When the film ________ , we ________ for a bus for half an hour.

6 Order the words to make sentences.

1 half / he / hour / ago / arrived / an
____
2 years / ten / built / house / ago / they / this
____
3 test / the / ago / minutes / we / started / fifteen
____
4 months / two / Ed / Sue / and / holiday / on / went / ago
____
5 teacher / we / ago / weeks / got / three / new / a
____

Speaking language practice

7 Complete the dialogues with the words below.

do fan free go hang into keen play what

1 A: ________ are your hobbies and interests?
B: I often ________ swimming.
2 A: What do you in your ________ time?
B: I ________ video games.
3 A: What do you enjoy doing in the evenings?
B: I ________ out with my friends.
4 A: Are you ________ sport?
B: I'm a big ________ of basketball.
5 A: Do you ________ much sport?
B: No, I'm not very ________ on sport.

1 Match photos A–E with words 1–5.

A

B

C

D

E

1 [C] presenter
2 [ ] field
3 [ ] netball
4 [ ] rugby
5 [ ] fan

2 Read the descriptions and complete the words.

1 This is when two countries fight: **w***a r*
2 This is where you can play football: **p**_ _ _ _
3 This number in words: 1,000,000,000: one **b**_ _ _ _ _ _
4 This describes the traditional sport of a country: **n**_ _ _ _ _ _ _ sport
5 Another word for *road*: **s**_ _ _ _ _

3 Complete the sentences with words from Exercises 1 and 2.

1 Last year there were vegetables here but now the *field* is empty.
2 Cycling is one of France's __________ sports.
3 I'm a big __________ of my town's football team.
4 The team are on the __________ . They're getting ready for the match.
5 The sports __________ on this TV programme is one of my dad's friends.
6 __________ is a good sport for tall people!

4 Match one word from A with one word from B to make word friends. Match the word friends with the photos.

A get (x2) join the ~~keep~~ kick the throw the

B ball (x2) ~~fit~~ game hurt tired

1 *keep fit*

2 __________

3 __________

4 __________

5 __________

6 __________

5 Complete the sentences with the Past Simple form of the verbs in brackets.

1 Terry *pushed* (push) Dave and *scored* (score) a goal.
2 The fans __________ (support) their team at the match.
3 The game __________ (continue) after a short break.
4 Jake __________ (get) hurt in the rugby game.
5 The English __________ (take) football to Argentina.
6 They __________ (make) some new rules for the sport.
7 The first game of football __________ (be) probably in England, hundreds of years ago.

6 **Read the video script. Underline any words or phrases you don't know and find their meaning in your dictionary.**

Rugbynet

There are many ball sports. In football, the players kick the ball. In netball, they throw the ball. In rugby, they run with the ball. Sometimes they push players to get the ball. There is another interesting ball sport. It's got a very big net, but the players use a rugby ball. There are some rules from netball and some rules from rugby. It's called rugbynetball or rugbynet. People think this is a completely new sport, but it isn't. It started about a hundred years ago. It's a fast game and rugby players like it a lot. The presenter wants to try. He joins the game. Some of the players are very big, but he's very small. It's hard. They run, they throw. Is it a goal? No, it isn't. There aren't many rules, and players can run everywhere. And they can try to take the ball. It's like a fight. Now the presenter's got the ball. He runs, he throws. He's fast, he's good. Rugbynet is fast and dangerous. The players get tired and they sometimes get hurt. But they love it and say it's fun!

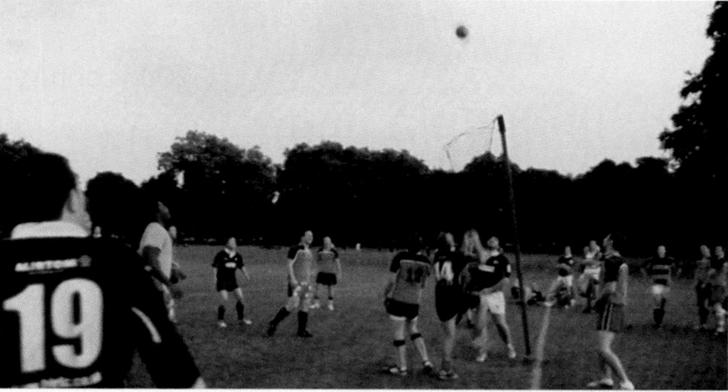

7 The time machine

VOCABULARY
Talking about history | Technology, internet and computers | Everyday technology

GRAMMAR
Past Simple negative (regular and irregular verbs) | Past Simple questions and short answers (regular and irregular verbs)

READING
Losing a favourite gadget

LISTENING
Childhood

SPEAKING
Agreeing and disagreeing

WRITING
A personal email with news

BBC CULTURE
Are museums boring?

7.1 VOCABULARY The past and technology

I can talk about technology and important moments in the past.

1 ● **When did these things happen? Look at the pictures and complete the sentences.**

1 Life was hard *in the Middle Ages* .

2 My sister was born ______ ago.

3 I went to England ______ .

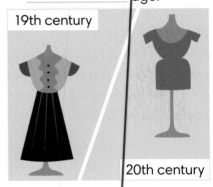

4 Fashion changed a lot ______ .

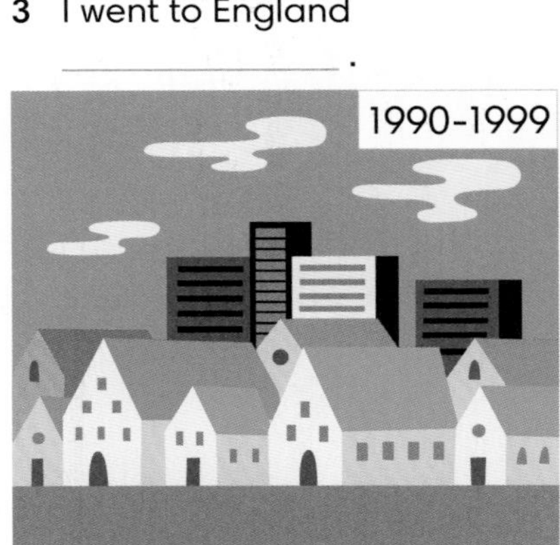

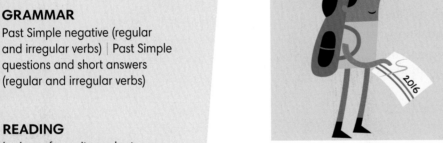

5 Our town changed a lot ______ .

6 Phones looked very different ______ .

2 ● **Complete the words in the sentences.**

1 The bicycle was a very important i*n v ent i o*n.
2 Darwin's t_ _ _r_ of evolution wasn't popular at first.
3 Scientists believe that the u_ _ _ _r_e started with the Big Bang, thirteen billion years ago.
4 John Blankenbaker invented the p_ _ _ _ _ _ c_ _ _ _ _ _r. The monitor was like a television and the keyboard was very, very big.
5 There was a fire and a big e_ _ _o_ _ _n in the factory.

3 ●● **Complete the sentences with the Past Simple form of the verbs below.**

become begin buy can eat ~~sell~~ understand write

1 Last week my dad *sold* his car for a lot of money.
2 I __________ everything the teacher said.
3 We __________ an essay in class yesterday.
4 James __________ a big piece of cake and was ill on his birthday.
5 I __________ swim when I was eight years old.
6 Sue __________ a good dictionary last week.
7 The concert __________ at 8.00 and finished at 11.00.
8 My sister Katy __________ a teacher in 2016.

4 ● **Complete the word puzzle with technology words. What's the hidden word?**

	[1] *n*	*e*	*t*	*w*	*o*	*r*	*k*	*i*	*n*	*g*
				e						
		2								
3										
	4									
5										
				e						

1 You can use this site to post photos, read friends' news and chat with friends: social __________ site
2 A video camera on your computer; you can use it to have video calls with friends: __________
3 This is the program that shows the internet on your screen: web __________
4 This is a website that helps you find information on the internet: search __________
5 You can use this to call your friends. It usually has a camera for photos and videos and you can also get on the internet with it: __________

The hidden word is: __________ .

5 ●● **Complete the sentences with words from Exercise 4 in the correct form.**

1 I'm on several *social networking sites* and check them all the time.
2 My favourite __________ is Google.
3 With my __________ , I can see my friends when we chat online.
4 I often use the Wikipedia __________ to get information for school.
5 I've got a new __________ and I love it! It's so thin and the batteries last a long time.
6 My dad uses Firefox but my favourite __________ is Google Chrome.

6 ●● **Find words in the word search below to complete the sentences. Look ↑, ↓, ↗ and ↘.**

1 Albert Einstein's *theory* of relativity is very important.
2 The Past Simple of *sell* is __________ .
3 I use a web __________ to search online.
4 YouTube is my favourite __________ .
5 I __________ too much and my tummy hurts.
6 I can message you on Skype but I haven't got a __________ , so I can't see you.
7 I __________ swim when I was three.

T	N	M	N	T	A	O	R	W	S	R
D	Q	B	V	C	S	R	S	K	J	I
I	M	S	W	I	T	P	N	T	C	C
B	J	M	O	L	E	A	R	G	A	O
T	K	H	I	(T	H	E	O	R	Y)	U
Z	N	I	A	T	T	V	A	O	E	L
E	T	A	I	I	U	H	V	F	P	D
K	P	I	S	O	L	D	S	F	S	P
G	L	B	O	C	L	Q	U	S	U	E
W	E	B	C	A	M	D	R	N	I	V
W	L	B	R	O	W	S	E	R	S	A

7 ●●● **Complete the blog with one word in each gap.**

myblog

My high-tech grandma

It was my gran's birthday three days [1] *ago* . She was born in [2] __________ 1950s. When she was young, there weren't any personal [3] __________ , so she wrote letters, not emails or texts. Now she loves technology. She's very interested in Greek myths, and her favourite [4] __________ is greekmyth.com. My present for her birthday was a [5] __________ so that she can see her sister in Australia when they chat online. My parents' present was a new [6] __________ ! It's really cool and the batteries last forever! [7] __________ to them she can now text and send messages easily. I tried to explain social [8] __________ sites to her but it was hard!

7.2 GRAMMAR Past Simple (negative)

I can use the Past Simple negative to talk about events in the past.

1 ● **Match pictures A–F with sentences 1–6.**

A
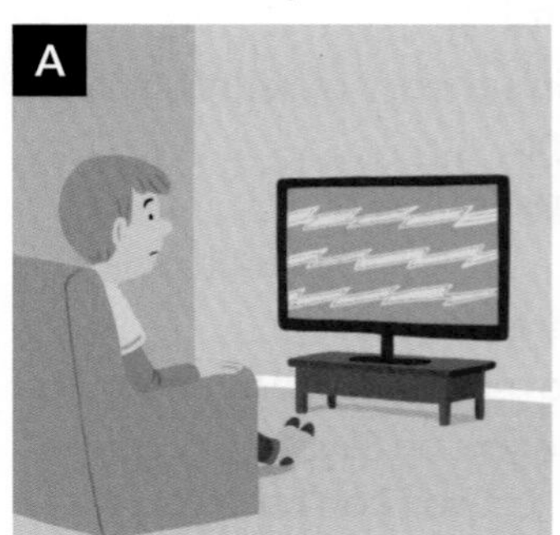

B

C

D

E
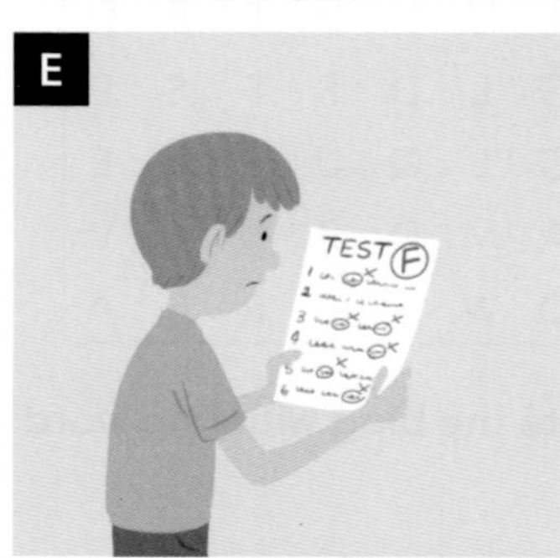

F

1 [C] I didn't understand the question.
2 [ ] I didn't watch the film.
3 [ ] I didn't have a shower.
4 [ ] I didn't win the cup.
5 [ ] I didn't sleep.
6 [ ] I didn't pass the test.

2 ● **Make the sentences negative.**

1 I played tennis yesterday.
I didn't play tennis yesterday.
2 Jack went to the USA on holiday.
____
3 My parents bought an expensive TV last week.
____
4 We had a test in class this morning.
____
5 I chatted to my friends on a social networking site last night.
____
6 Tanya lost her smartphone at the weekend.
____

3 ●● **Write sentences about Pete using the Past Simple form of the verbs in brackets.**

1 (get up late ✓)
On Saturday Pete got up late.
2 (have eggs for breakfast ✗)
He didn't have eggs for breakfast.
3 (do his homework ✗)
____
4 (go shopping ✓)
____
5 (hang out with his friends ✗)
____
6 (play a computer game ✓)
____
7 (have dinner with his parents ✗)
____
8 (stay up late ✗)
____

4 ●●● **Complete the text with the Past Simple form of the verbs below.**

~~be~~ buy eat go have like not go not have not like not see not spend see stay take walk watch

When I [1] *was* in England, I [2] ______ with my English friend Jenny and she [3] ______ me to London for a weekend. We [4] ______ shopping but we [5] ______ to some interesting museums. One was very big and I [6] ______ some amazing things there. They [7] ______ lots of things from Egypt. We [8] ______ everything because it was so big and we [9] ______ much time. There was a small shop there and I [10] ______ some postcards, but I [11] ______ a lot of money. Then we [12] ______ through a lovely park and [13] ______ the boats on the River Thames. There was a food market and we [14] ______ some fish and chips. I [15] ______ the fish but I [16] ______ the chips – they were cold.

7.3 READING and VOCABULARY — Living without a smartphone

I can find specific detail in an article and talk about losing a favourite gadget.

1 Complete the words.

1 This keeps food and drinks cold: **f**r i d g e
2 You can boil water in this: **k**_ _ _ _ _
3 You use this so your mobile phone keeps working: **c**_ _ _ _ _ _
4 This cleans your teeth very well: **e**_ _ _ _ _ _ _ **t**_ _ _ _ _ _ _ _ _
5 You prepare hot meals on this: **c**_ _ _ _ _
6 You clean clothes in this: **w**_ _ _ _ _ _ **m**_ _ _ _ _ _

2 Read the article. Choose the best title.

a A day in London without a phone
b Why we love our phones
c A silly mistake on a train

3 Read the article again. Mark the sentences ✓ (right), ✗ (wrong) or ? (doesn't say).

1 ☐ Carly lost her phone at a café in London.
2 ☐ She travelled to London with classmates.
3 ☐ Someone took her phone from her pocket.
4 ☐ She didn't use her phone that day.
5 ☐ Her dad is buying her the newest phone for her birthday.
6 ☐ She missed her phone a lot.

A reader, Carly, tells us about losing her smartphone and how it felt!

OK, Carly, tell us about your smartphone. What happened?

It was the worst thing! I lost my smartphone a month ago when I went to London with the school. We went by train and I used it on the journey – to check emails and texts. I didn't use it a lot – only three or four times. Then when we were at a café in London, I wanted to send a message to my friend; my phone wasn't in my bag and it wasn't in my pocket! Disaster! I remembered I put it on a seat on the train and didn't put it back in my bag. Oops!

So, you checked with the train company, right?

Of course! But they didn't have it. No, someone saw it and thought, 'What a nice phone!' and put it in their bag or pocket! It was expensive and I didn't have the money to buy another one. I waited for a week and then asked my dad. He bought me a cheap one, but it's my birthday next month, so I'm hoping!

Was that week hard?

It was terrible. I talked to my friends on my mum's phone and used my computer for emails but I hated it. I didn't sleep, lessons were hard at school – it was very strange. People say we use our phones too much – I think they're right. Your phone becomes a part of you and that isn't right! But it's hard to live without them.

Past Simple (questions and short answers)

I can use the Past Simple to ask and answer questions about the past.

1 Complete the dialogue with the phrases below. OUT of class

Of course not! Seriously?

Tony: It rained every day when we were on holiday.
Gail: [1]__________ Every day?
Tony: Yes. It started the moment we got off the plane and it didn't stop.
Gail: Did you stay in the hotel room all week?
Tony: [2]__________ We went swimming in the rain. It was fun!

2 ● Write questions.

1 He lived in Scotland when he was young.
Did he live in Scotland when he was young?
2 All the students passed the test.
____
3 Maria found her essay.
____
4 They made a lot of noise last night.
____
5 Mick woke his parents up when he got home.
____
6 Chris and Sandy bought a new computer at the weekend.
____
7 Gary lost his smartphone at the concert.
____

3 ● Write short answers for the questions in Exercise 2.

1 ✓ *Yes, he did.*
2 ✗ __________
3 ✓ __________
4 ✗ __________
5 ✓ __________
6 ✓ __________
7 ✗ __________

4 ●● Read the answers. Write questions about the parts in bold.

1 The party finished **at midnight**.
When did the party finish?
2 Sarah **went shopping** after school yesterday.
____
3 They built this house **in 2012**.
____
4 I lived **in Paris** in 2015.
____
5 I emailed **John** this morning.
____
6 Jenna watched **a comedy** on TV last night.
____

5 ●●● Complete the dialogue with the Past Simple form of the verbs in brackets.

Liam: Hi! Are you a new student here?
Molly: Yes, very new!
Liam: When [1]*did you start* (you/start)?
Molly: My first lesson was three days ago. We moved here from France.
Liam: When [2]__________ (you/move)?
Molly: Last month. It's very different here.
Liam: I'm sure! Are you French? You haven't got an accent.
Molly: No, my dad had a job in France.
Liam: Really? What [3]__________ (he/do) in France?
Molly: He taught English at the university.
Liam: Interesting! [4]__________ (you/like) France?
Molly: Oh yes. We were in Paris – it's a fantastic city.
Liam: We went there on holiday. It's beautiful.
Molly: [5]__________ (you/enjoy) the food?
Liam: I loved it! So, where [6]__________ (you/live) in Paris? Was it near the Eiffel Tower? Oh I'm sorry – I always ask too many questions!
Molly: That's OK!

7.5 LISTENING and VOCABULARY Childhood

I can identify specific detail in a radio interview and talk about my childhood.

1 Match pictures A–G with words 1–7.

1 [E] CD
2 [ ] ringtone
3 [ ] earphones
4 [ ] DVD
5 [ ] games console
6 [ ] MP3 player
7 [ ] tracks

2 Match the comments with words from Exercise 1.

1 I've got a new one. It's really loud and everyone on the train looked at me when it started this morning! *ringtone*

2 Nathan is always using it. His head and his fingers hurt but he still continues! ________

3 There are sixteen on his new album. My favourite is the last one. It's brilliant. ________

4 My dad's got hundreds of them – mainly music from the 80s and 90s. ________

5 In my bedroom I don't wear them but when I'm out, I do. ________

6 I haven't got any. I watch all my films online now. ________

7 You can get more music on it than on a phone and it's really small, so you can put it in your pocket. ________

3 16 **Listen to an interview. Match the speakers (1–4) with the questions they are answering (a–h).**

1 [ ] [ ] Beth
2 [ ] [ ] Becky
3 [ ] [ ] Charlie
4 [ ] [ ] Lisa

a Where did you meet your first best friend?
b Did you live near him or her?
c Were your hobbies and interests the same?
d Did you like the same music?
e What toys did you like?
f Did you like the same food?
g Did you dress in a similar way?
h Is he or she still your best friend today?

Beth

Becky

Charlie

Lisa

4 16 **Listen again. Choose the correct option.**

1 Beth and Eva met at *primary* / *secondary* school.
2 They had *the same* / *different* interests.
3 Gwen and Becky are *no longer* / *still* friends.
4 They *liked* / *didn't like* the same music.
5 Ben and Charlie *lived* / *didn't live* next to each other.
6 They wore *different* / *similar* clothes.
7 Lisa and Tina liked *boys'* / *girls'* toys.
8 They liked the *same* / *different* food.

I can agree and disagree with statements.

OUT of class

1 **Choose the correct option.**

1 That's not *well* / *fair*!
2 It was a *hurt* / *pain* in the neck.

2 **Match sentences a–b with phrases 1–2 from Exercise 1.**

a ☐ We arrived first but the people at that table got their meal before us!
b ☐ The shop near our home was closed, so I cycled all the way into town to the supermarket.

3 **Order the words to make phrases for agreeing and disagreeing.**

1 agree / yes / I
Yes, I agree.
2 so / think / too / I
____
3 but / agree / I / sorry / don't
____
4 sure / not / I'm
____
5 agree / don't / I
____
6 right / that's
____
7 right / maybe / you're
____
8 disagree / but / sorry / I
____
9 true / that's / perhaps
____

4 **Complete the dialogues with one or two words in each gap.**

1 A: I think the correct answer is D.
B: Sorry but I *don't* agree.
2 A: That blue bag is the perfect present for Jan.
B: Maybe you're __________ , but I prefer the red one.
3 A: I think it's a good idea to meet before the cinema.
B: I think __________ too.
4 A: We can get the bus. It stops right outside Diana's house.
B: Yes, __________ right.
5 A: Vegetarian food is very healthy.
B: Perhaps that's __________ , but it's sometimes very boring.
6 A: Katy is the best student at Maths in the school.
B: I'm not __________ . Benji Sanders is also really good.
7 A: The best track on the new album is *Clouds*.
B: Sorry but I __________ . I think it's *She's in the Past*.

5 **Complete the dialogue with sentences a–e.**

Jo: This is the best holiday ever!
Liz: [1]c It's amazing! I'm glad we came here.
Jo: But it's really hot today. It's too hot to sit on the beach. It isn't good for us.
Liz: [2]___ But I still love sunbathing!
Jo: But we were on the beach yesterday and the day before. Let's go into town today.
Liz: [3]___ Let me think. No, I want to relax.
Jo: We can relax tomorrow! We can go shopping or visit the museum. It's a good way to spend an afternoon!
Liz: [4]___ That isn't a good idea. We can go shopping and visit museums when we're home!
Jo: [5]___ I agree with you. But this is a new country, a new town and a new museum! Come on!

a Yes, that's right.
b I'm not sure.
c I think so too.
d Sorry but I don't agree.
e Perhaps that's true.

7.7 WRITING An email

I can write a personal email with news.

1 Read the email and tick the things Claire writes about.

1 ☑ a party
2 ☐ a present
3 ☐ a short holiday
4 ☐ the weather
5 ☐ activities on the holiday
6 ☐ food on holiday
7 ☐ a new pet

From: Claire;
To: Mason;

[1] *Hi* Mason,

[2] ________ are you? Did your birthday party [3] ________ OK? Sorry I was away!

[4] ________ the weekend we stayed with my aunt and cousins in Scotland. They've got a great house by a lake. On Saturday we [5] ________ for a long walk with their dogs. [6] ________, on Sunday, we visited an art gallery with lots of old pictures of Scotland. It was really interesting.

[7] ________ what! I've got a new dog! When we got home last night, my dad took me to his friend's house. Their dog had puppies and they gave me one! He's so cute!

[8] ________ you soon!

Lots of [9] ________,

Claire

2 Complete the email with the words below.

at go guess ~~hi~~ how love see then went

3 Write the phrases below in the correct category.

~~After that we went to town.~~ Guess what! Hi Katya! How are you? Kisses, Phone me! Lots of love, Love and hugs, Write back soon! Then we went round a museum. See you soon. Did your test go OK? I stayed with my friend.

Greetings: ________
Ask for news: ________, ________
Give your news: *After that we went to town.*, ________, ________
Give some surprising news: ________
Endings: ________, ________, ________, ________, ________, ________

4 Read the writing task and the questions below. Make some notes.

Your friend was recently in a competition. Write an email to him/her asking about the competition. Give your own news and add something surprising or interesting.

What sort of competition?

____

What did you do last week?

____

What's your surprising news?

____

5 Write your email. Remember to do these things.

- Use Claire's email to help you.
- Start and end your email with appropriate phrases.
- Use the phrases for asking for and giving news in Exercise 3.

7.8 SELF-ASSESSMENT

For each learning objective, tick (✓) the box that best matches your ability.

☺☺ = I understand and can help a friend.

☹ = I understand but have some questions.

☺ = I understand and can do it by myself.

☹☹ = I do not understand.

		☺☺	☺	☹	☹☹	Need help?	Now try ...
7.1	Vocabulary					Students' Book pp. 82–83 Workbook pp. 78–79	Ex. 1–3, p. 87
7.2	Grammar					Students' Book p. 84 Workbook p. 80	Ex. 4, p. 87
7.3	Reading					Students' Book p. 85 Workbook p. 81	
7.4	Grammar					Students' Book p. 86 Workbook p. 82	Ex. 5, p. 87
7.5	Listening					Students' Book p. 87 Workbook p. 83	
7.6	Speaking					Students' Book p. 88 Workbook p. 84	Ex. 6, p. 87
7.7	Writing					Students' Book p. 89 Workbook p. 85	

7.1 I can talk about technology and important moments in the past.
7.2 I can use the Past Simple negative to talk about events in the past.
7.3 I can find specific detail in an article and talk about losing a favourite gadget.
7.4 I can use the Past Simple to ask and answer questions about the past.
7.5 I can identify specific detail in a radio interview and talk about my childhood.
7.6 I can agree and disagree with statements.
7.7 I can write a personal email with news.

What can you remember from this unit?

New words I learned (the words you most want to remember from this unit)	**Expressions and phrases I liked** (any expressions or phrases you think sound nice, useful or funny)	**English I heard or read outside class** (e.g. from websites, books, adverts, films, music)

7.9 SELF-CHECK

Vocabulary

1 Complete the words.

1 Use this when your hair is wet: **h**_ _ _ _ _ _ _ _ _
2 Use this to boil water: **k**_ _ _ _ _
3 Use this to see people when you chat online: **w**_ _ _ _ _
4 Use this to clean your teeth: **e**_ _ _ _ _ _ _ **t**_ _ _ _ _ _ _ _ _
5 Use these to play music for yourself so other people can't hear: **e**_ _ _ _ _ _ _ _ _
6 Use this to store and listen to music: **M**_ _ **p**_ _ _ _ _
7 Use this to call your friends and to go on the internet: **s**_ _ _ _ _ _ _ _ _ _

2 Order the letters and write the words in the sentences.

1 I like it when we do experiments in Science lessons but I don't understand the ________ (reyhot).
2 My ________ (treginno) is the same as yours – every time your phone rings, I think it's mine.
3 Do you like the first ________ (catkr) on the band's new album?
4 My clothes are dirty – I need to put them in the ________ (gwnaish emcahin).
5 My dad bought me a new games ________ (sloceon) for my birthday. Come and try it with me.
6 Which ________ (toninevin) was the most important of the last century?
7 Facebook is my favourite social ________ (tneogwrikn) site.
8 I always use a search ________ (eening) like Google to find what I need.

3 Complete the sentences with the verbs below.

became could sold thought understood wrote

1 I ________ fifteen emails and ten texts this morning.
2 The teacher explained the new word and I ________ easily.
3 My uncle first ________ ill a year ago.
4 My brother ________ speak Italian very well when we lived in Italy but he can't now.
5 I ________ the meeting was at 4.00. Sorry I'm late.
6 Jan's parents ________ their house in London and moved to Scotland.

Grammar

4 Make sentences in the Past Simple.

1 I / not do / my English homework but I / do / my Maths homework
____
2 I / eat / the meat but I / not eat / the vegetables
____
3 Ella / go / to Mike's party but she / not go to Henry's party
____
4 we / have / Biology today but we / not have / History
____
5 my parents / not learn / French at school but they / learn / English
____

5 Read the answers. Write questions about the parts in bold.

1 We got home from London **at midnight**.
____
2 In London we stayed **at the Grand Hotel**.
____
3 We met **Jack** in Trafalgar Square.
____
4 I had **fish and chips** for dinner.
____
5 We travelled to London and back **by train**.
____

Speaking language practice

6 Complete the dialogues with one word in each gap.

1 A: This is really difficult.
B: I think ________ too.
2 A: Let's finish now and have a break.
B: OK, ________ you're right.
3 A: This is a fantastic film.
B: I ________ . It's rubbish!
4 A: Is your house number 54?
B: That's ________ .
5 A: I think the answer is B.
B: I'm not ________ . It may be C.
6 A: The cake at Sunny's café is the best in town.
B: Sorry, but I don't ________ . The cake at Weston's is the best!

1 Look at the pictures and complete the crossword.

1
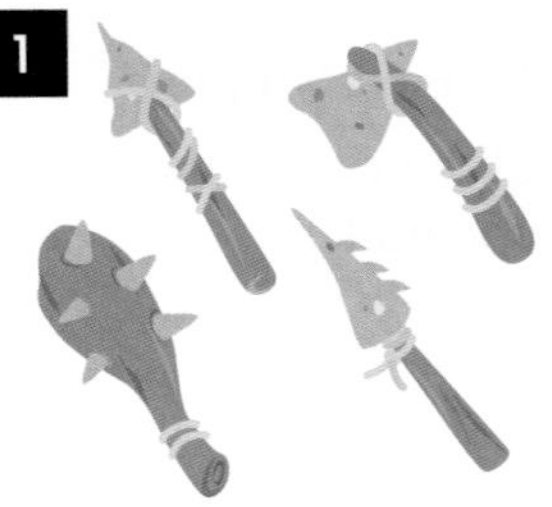

2

3
1,000,000

4

5
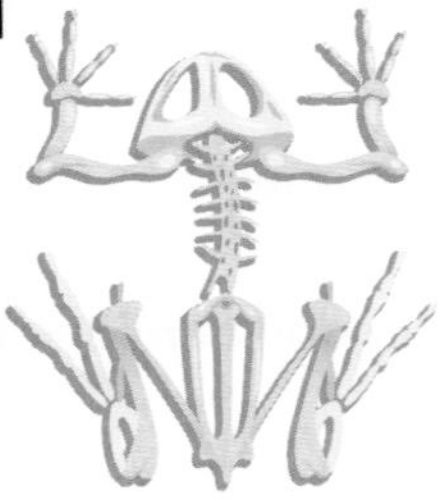

6

2 Order the letters and write the words in the sentences.

1 There are some interesting new *exhibits* (tixsheib) at the museum this week.
2 When the dinosaur came __________ (evali) in the film, it was very funny.
3 You don't pay here – it's __________ (refe).
4 Someone threw a __________ (noste) at our car! Now the window's broken!
5 There is a statue of Theodore Roosevelt, the American __________ (depersnit), at the museum.
6 I can't come out now. We've got a __________ (rvoitsi) – my aunt from London.

3 Match photos A–F with words 1–6.

A

B

C

D

E
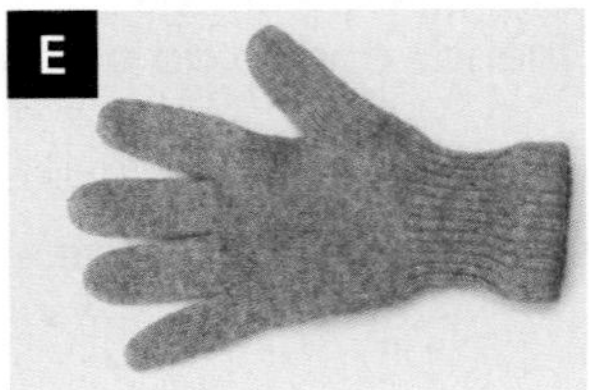

F

1 [F] diamond
2 [ ] glove
3 [ ] policeman
4 [ ] electricity
5 [ ] airport
6 [ ] fire

4 Complete the sentences with the words below.

crime fake murderer policeman ~~robbery~~ weapon

1 There was a *robbery* at the bank in town last week. They lost millions of pounds!
2 A gun is a __________ .
3 My brother is a __________ and he works in London.
4 This picture isn't real – it's a __________ !
5 In the film, they find the __________ and put him in prison.
6 What he did was terrible! It was a terrible __________ and they must put him in prison!

5 Order the letters and write the words in the sentences.

1 I don't like old furniture. I prefer *modern* (dronem) furniture.
2 These guns don't kill people. They only __________ (nuts) them.
3 The film has a sad ending. The two friends __________ (ide) in a car accident.
4 I don't play games on my __________ (tappol) – I only use it to look at websites or watch videos.
5 There are a lot of __________ (thixsibe) at the Black Museum.

6 **Read the video script. Underline any words or phrases you don't know and find their meaning in your dictionary.**

The Black Museum

Everyone knows the name New Scotland Yard. It's the home of the London Police. It's also the home of a special museum called The Crime Museum. People also call it the The Black Museum. There are things in here from the most terrible crimes of the last 150 years. A policeman called Percy Neame started this strange museum in 1875. He wanted new policemen to learn from the exhibits. The Crime Museum is usually only for policemen, but today people can see 600 exhibits from The Crime Museum here at the Museum of London. There are lots of guns. But there are also some unusual things. Here are the gloves of a terrible murderer. And this champagne is very old. The police found it in 1963 after the Great Train Robbery. There are some horrible weapons. And this is how some murderers died. Many exhibits are very old, but some are more modern. There's a police car from 1996. This isn't a mobile phone – it's a stun gun. It stops people with electricity. This laptop is from a fire at an airport in 2007. And look at this big diamond – cost: about 200 million pounds! The police stopped a robbery in 2000. They changed the real diamond with this one. It's a fake. These exhibits are certainly not boring.

Talking to the world

VOCABULARY
Geography

GRAMMAR
Modal verbs: *have to/don't have to, mustn't* | Articles: first and second mention

READING
Learning languages | Makaton

LISTENING
Communication

SPEAKING
Understanding

ENGLISH IN USE
Verb + preposition collocations

BBC CULTURE
Can you send postcards from Antarctica?

8.1 VOCABULARY Geography

I can talk about different countries.

1 Order the letters and write the words. Match them with 1–4 on the compass.

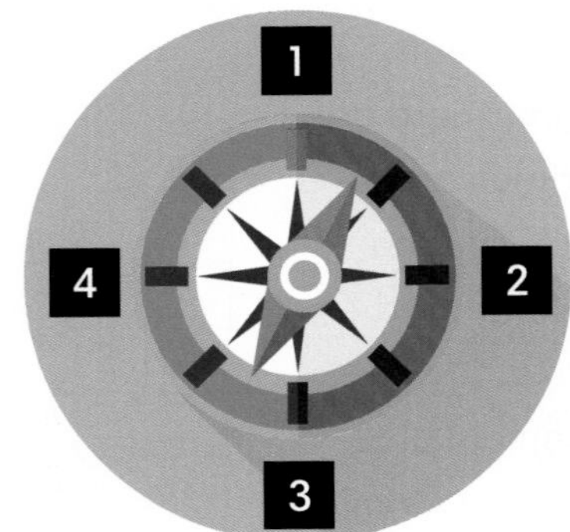

a [2] *east* (stae)
b [ ] ______ (husot)
c [ ] ______ (tronh)
d [ ] ______ (tsew)

2 Complete the instructions with words from Exercise 1.

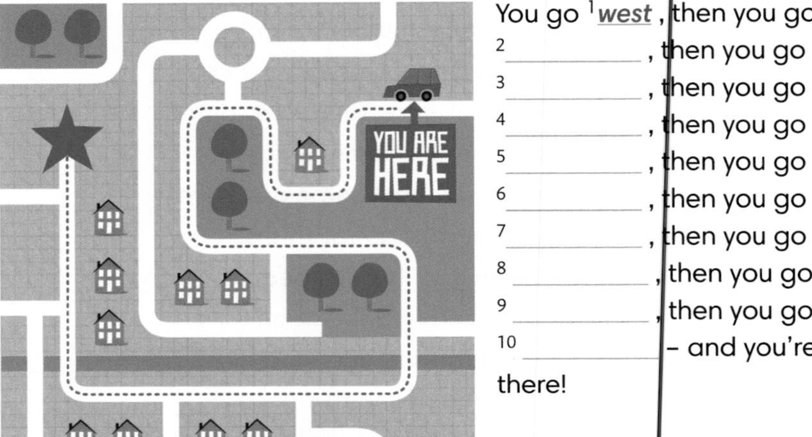

You go [1] *west* , then you go
[2] ______ , then you go
[3] ______ , then you go
[4] ______ , then you go
[5] ______ , then you go
[6] ______ , then you go
[7] ______ , then you go
[8] ______ , then you go
[9] ______ , then you go
[10] ______ – and you're there!

3 Match A–G on the map with continents 1–7.

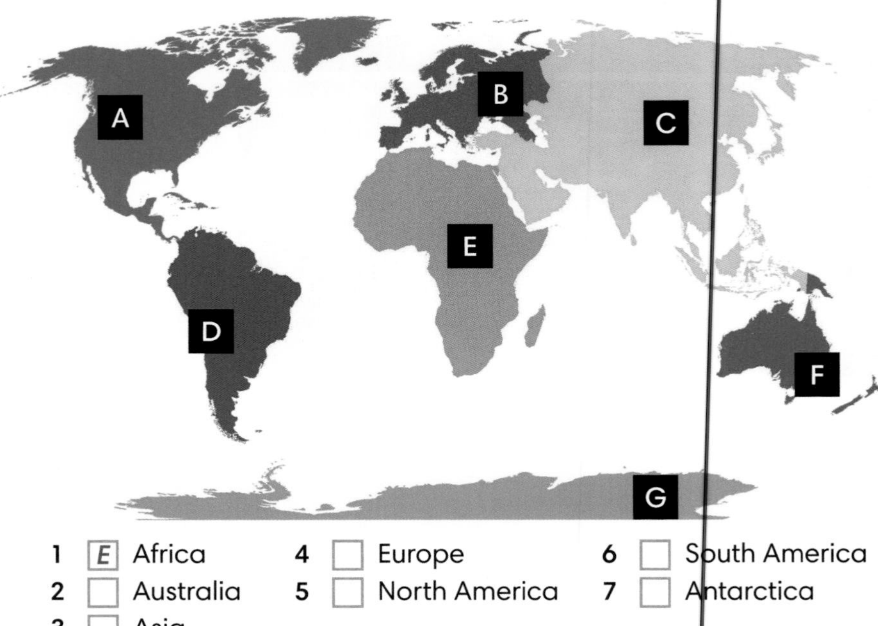

1 [E] Africa
2 [ ] Australia
3 [ ] Asia
4 [ ] Europe
5 [ ] North America
6 [ ] South America
7 [ ] Antarctica

4 ● Look at the picture and complete the words.

1 m*o u n t a i n*
2 r_ _ _ _
3 l_ _ _
4 i_ _ _ _ _
5 s_ _

5 ●● Complete the word puzzle with words from Exercise 4. What's the hidden word?

			[1] *m*	*o*	*u*	*n*	*t*	*a*	*i*	*n*
				c						
	[2]									
		[3]								
[4]										

1 We can go up this. It's very high.
2 We can cross this on a bridge.
3 We can swim here.
4 There's water all round this.

The hidden word is: __________ .

6 ● Match words 1–5 with examples a–e.

1	[c] capital city	a	$
2	[ ] language	b	150,000
3	[ ] flag	c	Paris
4	[ ] money	d	Italian
5	[ ] population	e	(flag)

7 ●● Complete the sentences with words 1-5 from Exercise 6.

1 We changed our *money* at the airport and I've now got lots and lots of Euros to spend on holiday.
2 The __________ of the UK is bigger now than ten years ago. It's over sixty-five million.
3 What __________ do they speak in Brazil?
4 The __________ of Australia is Canberra. I always thought it was Sydney.
5 There are fifty stars on the American __________ .

8 ●● Write the words in the sentences.

1 The Nile is the longest *r i v e r* in Africa.
2 _ _ _ _ _ is the opposite point on the compass from south.
3 The _ _ _ _ _ _ _ _ _ _ of Spain is over forty-five million.
4 The UK _ _ _ _ is red, white and blue.
5 There are some strange fish in the very deep parts of the _ _ _ _ _ .
6 _ _ _ _ _ _ _ _ _ _ is a big continent. Penguins live there.

9 ●●● Complete the text with the words below.

capital ~~country~~ Europe lake mountains population river sea south

My [1]*country*, England, is part of [2]__________ . I live in the [3]__________ of England and my house is only five minutes from the [4]__________ . We go there at the weekend and sit on the beach in the summer. On a clear day you can see France across the water. There aren't any [5]__________ in my area – it's very flat. But my house is near a long [6]__________ – my dad goes fishing there quite often! There's a [7]__________ near here too. We sometimes swim there and you can walk all round it – it takes about an hour. We live about an hour and a half from London, the [8]__________ city. It's a really big city – the [9]__________ is more than 8.5 million!

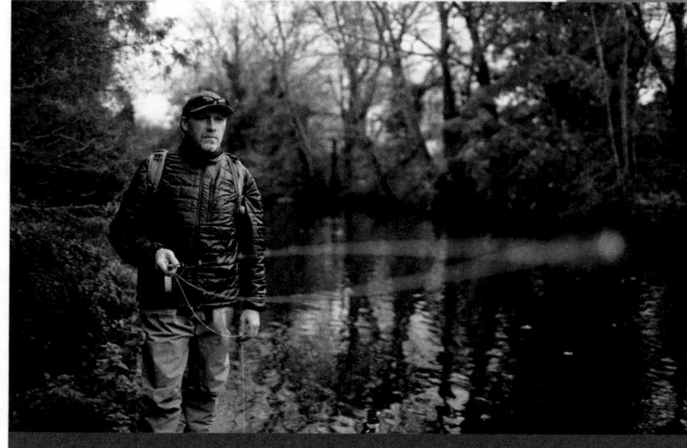

8.2 GRAMMAR Modal verbs: *have to/don't have to, mustn't*

I can use *have to/don't have to* and *mustn't to* talk about rules.

1 ● **Match pictures A–F with sentences 1–6.**

1 [C] You mustn't use mobile phones here.
2 [ ] You mustn't use this bridge.
3 [ ] You mustn't park on the grass.
4 [ ] You mustn't swim in this lake.
5 [ ] You mustn't open this before your birthday.
6 [ ] You mustn't drive fast here.

2 ● **Complete the sentences with the correct form of *have to*.**

1 a ✓ You *have to* be quiet in exams.
  b ✗ You *don't have to* be quiet at break time.
2 a ✓ I __________ do homework every evening.
  b ✗ I __________ do English homework every evening.
3 a ✓ My sister __________ tidy her room on Saturdays.
  b ✗ My sister __________ go shopping with my parents.
4 a ✓ We __________ do Maths tests every week.
  b ✗ We __________ go to school in the holidays.

3 ●● **Complete the sentences with *have to* or *don't have to*.**

1 I *don't have to* get up early on Saturdays. I can stay in bed until 11.00!
2 We __________ give our homework to the teacher on Tuesday mornings or she gets angry.
3 My friends __________ help with the housework. My mum says they're very lazy.
4 At our school you __________ wear a uniform. That's good – I like choosing my own clothes.
5 At my friend's school they __________ stand up when the teacher comes in. We don't.

4 ●● **Choose the correct option.**

1 You (*mustn't*) / *have to* / *don't have to* touch that. It's hot!
2 You *mustn't* / *have to* / *don't have to* buy the tickets online. There isn't a phone number.
3 You *mustn't* / *have to* / *don't have to* put the knife in your mouth when you eat. It's dangerous and rude!
4 We *mustn't* / *have to* / *don't have to* get the early train. The lessons start later today.
5 In the race, first they *mustn't* / *have to* / *don't have to* swim a long way, then run, then cycle!
6 We *mustn't* / *have to* / *don't have to* bring dictionaries to school. There are lots in the classroom.
7 Shh! Be quiet! You *mustn't* / *have to* / *don't have to* talk during the exam.
8 It's OK, you can go. You *mustn't* / *have to* / *don't have to* wait for me – I can come later.

5 ●●● **Complete the dialogue with *mustn't* or the correct form of *have to*.**

Tim: How's your summer job at the fast food restaurant?
Eve: It's OK. But there are so many rules!
Tim: Like what?
Eve: You [1]*have to* wear a silly hat when you're in the kitchen. You [2]__________ touch the food with your fingers.
Tim: Those aren't silly. They're important!
Eve: Mmm … We [3]__________ have a break for longer than fifteen minutes. We [4]__________ chat too long with the customers. And we [5]__________ start work at 7.30 in the morning! That's crazy!
Tim: But you [6]__________ do the job if you don't like it.
Eve: I [7]__________ earn some money, so yes, I do!
Tim: Well, you [8]__________ do *this* job. Look for another one. You can pick strawberries at the farm, like me.
Eve: Then you [9]__________ work all day in the hot sun. No, thank you!

8.3 **READING and VOCABULARY** Makaton

I can find specific detail in an article and talk about learning languages.

1 Complete the words in the sentences.

1 My English **v**o c a b u l a r y is not very good. I need to learn a lot more words.
2 At school my dad didn't learn a **f**_ _ _ _ _ _ language, but my mum learned French.
3 My cousin learned Spanish from Maria, a **n**_ _ _ _ _ speaker. Maria moved to England from Spain four years ago.
4 My aunt is German and my uncle is Australian. Their two children are **b**_ _ _ _ _ _ _ _, but they speak German better than English.
5 My dream is to speak English **f**_ _ _ _ _ _ _ and then work in England.
6 Finnish **g**_ _ _ _ _ _ is very difficult. I always confuse my tenses.

2 Read the article and mark the sentences T (true) or F (false).

1 ☐ Only British people use Makaton.
2 ☐ Three college students invented the language.
3 ☐ Makaton is for people who have problems communicating.
4 ☐ Many people use Makaton for a short time and then stop.
5 ☐ The name of the language is from the names of the researchers' children.

3 Read the article again. Answer the questions.

1 How many people use Makaton?

______

2 When did the three researchers invent Makaton?

______

3 Where did they work?

______

4 How many ideas can Makaton show?

______

5 What was the name of the male researcher?

______

6 Where did the letters in the name *Makaton* come from?

______

Makaton

Did you use Makaton when you were a child? Many people did. Today over 100,000 people, children and adults, use it in more than forty countries! So, what is Makaton? And which country speaks it?

In fact, it isn't a normal language. There isn't a country where people speak Makaton because it's an invented language. But it is very useful to a lot of people. In 1970 three researchers at the Royal College for Deaf People invented the language for people who had problems communicating. It was for people who couldn't hear, people who had learning problems, people who had problems communicating, and especially for young children who were slow learning to speak.

Makaton uses movements of the hand and body, and expressions on the face together with spoken words to communicate. It's possible to communicate more than 7,000 ideas! When the speaker starts to use spoken language (like a young child) he uses Makaton and words and then stops using Makaton completely. For other people with bigger problems, Makaton helps them 'talk' to other people. For example, it can help them take part in games, read and tell stories, and show how they are feeling.

Margaret Walker, Katherine Johnstone and Tony Cornforth created the language and their wonderful idea helps a lot of people today. The name of the language is the first letters of their names.

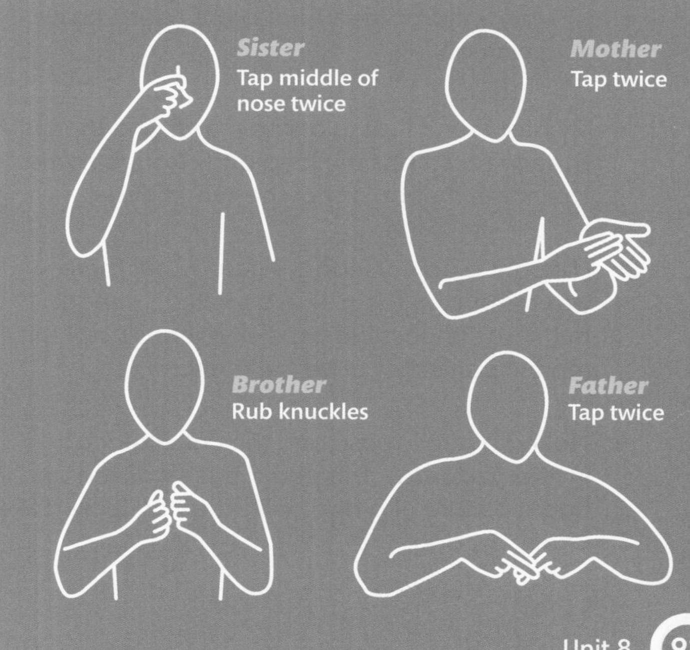

8.4 GRAMMAR Articles: first and second mention

I can use *a/an* and *the* to talk about places in town.

1 Complete the dialogue with the phrases below. OUT of class

Got it! What does it mean?

A: Jacky said, 'See you in ten.' [1]______
B: That's short for 'See you in ten minutes.'
A: Ah, OK. [2]______

2 Write *a* or *an* before the words.

1 *an* electric kettle
2 ___ holiday
3 ___ orange
4 ___ artist
5 ___ river
6 ___ ocean
7 ___ X
8 ___ flag

3 Find and correct the mistakes in the sentences.

1 My brother's got a new laptop. A laptop was very cheap.
The laptop was very cheap.

2 I got a card from Ronny for my birthday. The card has a picture of the mountain. I think the mountain is in Japan.
______

3 Jacky's dad works in a big office. An office has a big window and you can see a lovely garden. The garden has lots of trees and flowers.
______

4 We're having the test in class today. The test is about vocabulary!
______

5 A: There's a car outside our gate.
B: Who's in the car?
A: I can see a man and a woman. I know the man – it's my friend's dad but I don't know a woman.
______

6 My best friend lives in a small town. The town is in Greece and it has the long and strange name. The name means 'city of the sun' in Greek.
______

7 I bought a pair of jeans yesterday but there was a mark on them. I tried to clean a mark but it was impossible. I took the jeans back this morning and they gave me a refund.
______

8 I found a pencil case and the calculator at school yesterday. The pencil case was red and it had a picture of a dog on it. The dog looked like Bruno, my dog!
______

4 Choose the correct option.

1 There's (a) / *the* new girl in our class. *A / The* girl's brother is in Dan's class.
2 We went to Paris last month and we stayed at *a / the* hotel. *A / The* hotel had *a / the* big swimming pool and *a / the* lovely restaurant. We ate in *a / the* restaurant every evening.
3 Do you want *a / the* biscuit? *A / The* chocolate ones are delicious! Or there's *a / the* cake. I can cut you *a / the* piece.
4 I bought *a / the* new smartphone and *a / the* new bag yesterday. *A / The* smartphone was expensive but *a / the* bag was cheap.
5 Peter is *a / the* student. He lives in *a / the* flat with two friends. *A / The* flat is small but he likes it.

5 Complete the dialogue with *a*, *an* or *the*.

Sam: Did you have [1]*a* good day yesterday?
Alex: Yes, thanks. My friend Mason came down from London by train. [2]___ train was late as usual, but then Dad drove us to [3]___ beach near Branksome. [4]___ beach is very small but very quiet. It was empty and we had [5]___ great time. We took [6]___ boat out to [7]___ island and back, and then we had [8]___ barbecue on [9]___ beach. On [10]___ island there are lots of birds and we took a lot of photos.
Sam: Oh, can I see [11]___ photos?
Alex: Yes. Here's my dad with [12]___ bird on his head! [13]___ bird made a terrible noise and it frightened Lily, my sister.
Sam: Have you got [14]___ photo of Lily with [15]___ bird?
Alex: No, she was too scared!

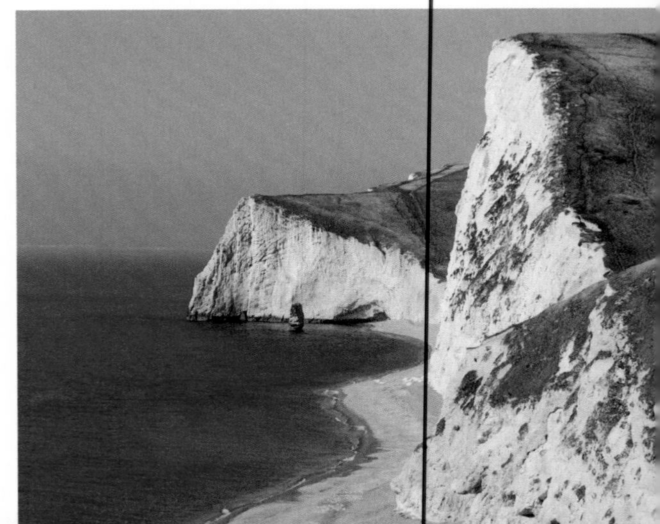

I can identify specific detail in a conversation and talk about communication.

1 Complete the sentences with the words below.

conversation letter ~~phone call~~ postcard Skype calls tweet

1 I got a late *phone call* from Dave last night.
2 It's better to have a face-to-face ______ about this, I think.
3 Please send me a ______ when you're on holiday, with a picture of your hotel on the front!
4 The school sent my mum a ______ about my test results. Look, it's in my bag.
5 Do you often have ______ with your friend in Norway?
6 When did you last ______ a comment?

2 WORD FRIENDS Choose the correct option.

1 I *made* / *(had)* a conversation with my dad about films.
2 I *sent* / *posted* a lot of text messages to my girlfriend.
3 I *made* / *sent* a couple of phone calls to my best friend.
4 I *called* / *asked* my mum some questions about my homework.
5 I *posted* / *sent* a message on Facebook about my party.
6 I *chatted* / *made* with a friend in France online.
7 I *posted* / *called* my uncle to ask him to help me fix my bike.

3 17 Listen. What sort of conversation are Beth and Lenny having? Choose the correct answer.

A

B

C

4 17 Listen again. Choose the correct answer.

1 At the moment Beth is
 a in her room.
 b in another room in her house.
 c in the garden.
2 Beth is there because
 a her computer is rubbish.
 b her brother's room is nicer.
 c there's bad wi-fi signal in other rooms.
3 For his birthday Lenny got a new
 a tablet.
 b camera.
 c smartphone.
4 Owen wants to
 a go to bed.
 b look at some pictures.
 c play some music.
5 Lenny agrees to
 a call Beth back.
 b give Owen some help.
 c help Beth with her guitar lesson.

8.6 SPEAKING Understanding

I can check if people understand me and say if I understand.

1 Complete the word in the informal greeting.

OUT of class

Hey, sw_ _ _ _e!

2 Order the words to make sentences.

1 see / you / do / ?
Do you see?
2 you / what / mean / do / ?
______
3 I / not / it / sure / get / I'm
______
4 understand / I / now
______
5 you / get / do / it / ?
______
6 what / you / mean / know / I / do / ?
______
7 understand / sorry / don't / I / I'm
______
8 see / I
______
9 right / oh
______
10 mean / you / 'email' / do / ?
______

3 Complete the dialogues with one word in each gap.

1 A: Click here and save the file.
B: Sorry, I don't get *it* .
2 A: The water has to be hotter to cook it. Do you ______ what I mean?
B: Oh, ______ .
3 A: Go along Broad Street and turn left, then right, then left and I'm on the right.
B: I ______ .
4 A: Let's buy two chicken and salad sandwiches.
B: Do you ______ two chicken sandwiches and two salads?
5 A: Click on the camera on the screen and you can see me!
B: I'm sorry I don't ______ .
6 A: ______ do you mean?
B: I mean click on 'Send' – here, you see?

4 Choose the correct answer.

Grandma: Sorry, Maggie. This Facebook is lovely but I'm not [1]___ I get it. How do I start it?
Maggie: OK, Gran, just click on the Facebook icon on the screen.
Grandma: Sorry, I don't [2]___ .
Maggie: OK, switch on your tablet.
Grandma: Wait a second. Right, I've got lots of little pictures of things.
Maggie: That's right. There's one with an 'F' on it. Touch that.
Grandma: Ah, I [3]___ – that's it. There's my picture. I want to send a message to Jenna. What do I do?
Maggie: Select Jenna from your friends.
Grandma: [4]___ do you mean?
Maggie: There's a picture of your friends. Touch that.
Grandma: Oh [5]___ . Now there are pictures of all the family!
Maggie: Yes, touch the picture of Jenna.
Grandma: Do you [6]___ the little picture of her face?
Maggie: That's right.
Grandma: OK.
Maggie: Now you can post a comment on her page. Or click 'Message' and send her a message.
Grandma: Now I get [7]___ . Thanks, darling.

	a	b	c
1	a see	(b) sure	c understand
2	a get	b mean	c understand
3	a see	b right	c now
4	a How	b Why	c What
5	a right	b see	c well
6	a understand	b mean	c think
7	a her	b on	c it

8.7 ENGLISH IN USE Verbs and prepositions

I can use verb + preposition collocations.

1 Complete the sentences with the verbs below. Add the correct prepositions.

learn look shout smile ~~talk~~ think

A

1 They are *talking about* a new film.

B

2 He is ________ a picture.

C

3 They are ________ History.

D

4 She is ________ Tom.

E

5 She is ________ Bill.

F

6 He is ________ Jo.

2 Match 1–6 with a–f to make sentences.

1 [b] Listen! My dad is shouting
2 [ ] Sorry, I can't talk now. I'm looking
3 [ ] My dad believes
4 [ ] I always worry
5 [ ] Last night I talked
6 [ ] Dan asked

a for extra chips.
b at my brother.
c to my friend for ages.
d for our hamster. It escaped!
e in hard work.
f about school exams.

3 Choose the correct answer.

1 I thought Tim was angry but then he smiled ___ me.
a for (b) at c about
2 Can you help me look ___ our cat?
a at b in c for
3 I talked ___ Robby about my computer and now it's fixed!
a for b about c to
4 My mum never shouted ___ us when we were young.
a at b in c for
5 You don't have to decide now. Think ___ it.
a for b about c in
6 This homework is hard and I want to ask the teacher ___ extra time.
a for b at c to

4 Complete the email with one word in each gap.

To: hello@sara.com

Hi Sara,

It was lovely to talk [1]*to* you on Skype yesterday. I hope you're enjoying your holiday! Mum and Dad are thinking [2]________ taking us to London for a few days. We can go to the Tate Modern. I love looking [3]________ all the pictures and sculptures there. I want to be an artist and at the Tate I can learn a lot [4]________ different artists. We can also go shopping in Oxford Street! I want to look [5]________ some winter boots. I asked [6]________ some for my birthday last month, but I didn't get them!

Let's Skype again soon and we can talk some more [7]________ your holiday. I love your new profile picture, by the way! Who are you smiling [8]________ ??

Speak soon,
Carole

8.8 SELF-ASSESSMENT

For each learning objective, tick (✓) the box that best matches your ability.

☺☺ = I understand and can help a friend.

☺ = I understand and can do it by myself.

☹ = I understand but have some questions.

☹☹ = I do not understand.

		☺☺	☺	☹	☹☹	Need help?	Now try ...
8.1	Vocabulary					Students' Book pp. 94–95 Workbook pp. 90–91	Ex. 1–2, p. 99
8.2	Grammar					Students' Book p. 96 Workbook p. 92	Ex. 4, p. 99
8.3	Reading					Students' Book p. 97 Workbook p. 93	
8.4	Grammar					Students' Book p. 98 Workbook p. 94	Ex. 5, p. 99
8.5	Listening					Students' Book p. 99 Workbook p. 95	
8.6	Speaking					Students' Book p. 100 Workbook p. 96	Ex. 6, p. 99
8.7	English in use					Students' Book p. 101 Workbook p. 97	Ex. 3, p. 99

8.1 I can talk about different countries.
8.2 I can use *have to/don't have to* and *mustn't* to talk about rules.
8.3 I can find specific detail in an article and talk about learning languages.
8.4 I can use *a/an* and *the* to talk about places in town.
8.5 I can identify specific detail in a conversation and talk about communication.
8.6 I can check if people understand me and say if I understand.
8.7 I can use verb + preposition collocations.

What can you remember from this unit?

New words I learned (the words you most want to remember from this unit)	**Expressions and phrases I liked** (any expressions or phrases you think sound nice, useful or funny)	**English I heard or read outside class** (e.g. from websites, books, adverts, films, music)

8.9 SELF-CHECK

Vocabulary

1 Match questions 1–6 with answers a–f.

1 ☐ What's the capital city of the USA?
2 ☐ What colours are on the French flag?
3 ☐ What's the highest mountain in the world?
4 ☐ Where do penguins live?
5 ☐ Which is the biggest ocean?
6 ☐ Which direction is the Arctic?

a Mount Everest.
b Red, white and blue.
c Washington DC.
d Antarctica.
e North.
f Pacific.

2 Complete the words in the sentences.

1 My cousin speaks Italian **f**_ _ _ _ _ _ _ because he lived in Italy when he was younger.
2 I **m**_ _ _ five phone calls but all my friends were out.
3 Jack **p**_ _ _ _ _ a really funny message on Facebook yesterday.
4 English isn't Katya's **n**_ _ _ _ _ language but she speaks it really well.
5 The **c**_ _ _ _ _ _ city of Scotland is Edinburgh.
6 I **s**_ _ _ a text to Jodie to say that we're in the café. I think she's coming.

3 Complete the sentences with the prepositions below.

about (x2) at for (x2) to

1 We learned ________ King Henry VIII at school today.
2 I asked the waiter ________ some bread and butter.
3 My friend shouted ________ me when I broke her phone.
4 Brad is very quiet. I don't know what he's thinking ________ .
5 Amy lost her homework. She looked ________ it for an hour.
6 We talked ________ Jim in the café this afternoon.

Grammar

4 Complete the note with the correct form of *have to*, *don't have* to or *mustn't*.

Mark,

I'm out until 7.30, remember? Your dinner's in the fridge; you [1] ________ do much – just put it in the microwave. It [2] ________ heat for five minutes.

Jim phoned – you [3] ________ miss football practice tonight. It's important!

You [4] ________ take the dog for a walk because Sue took him this afternoon, but you [5] ________ tidy your room. It's a mess!

Oh yes, and you [6] ________ finish your History project. It's nearly Friday!

And you [7] ________ forget to feed the dog at 6.30.

See you later!
Mum x

5 Complete the sentences with *a*/*an* or *the*.

1 Carl bought _____ new car yesterday. _____ car is red.
2 There's _____ new cinema and _____ old cinema in town. _____ new cinema is big and _____ old cinema is small.
3 _____ man is walking down the road. There's _____ dog with _____ man.
4 There's _____ bicycle outside the house. I think _____ bicycle is Helen's.
5 They built _____ new road in town. You can take _____ road to get to the country quicker.

Speaking language practice

6 Choose the correct option.

1 You've got a computer virus. Do you *find* / *understand* what I mean?
2 Oh *see* / *right*! Now I get *it* / *for*! I click this and I get on the website.
3 I'm not *right* / *sure* I understand. Can you repeat that?
4 Great! *Then* / *Now* I understand!
5 You can't do that on this forum. Do you *mean* / *see*?
6 It's not too late! What do you *think* / *mean*? It's only six o'clock.

1 Complete the words in the sentences.

1 We've got a new dog. He's very small and very **c**u t e .
2 My dad bought a book online. It was expensive because it's **r**_ _ _ and you can't often find it.
3 It's hot today. That's **u**_ _ _ _ _ _ because it's December!
4 The guitar is a **p**_ _ _ _ _ _ instrument at school and lots of my friends play it.
5 That picture is very good. I want to touch the bird in it! It's so **r**_ _ _!
6 I watched a new programme on TV last night. It was **b**_ _ _ _ _ _ _ _! I loved it.

2 Match 1–6 with a–f to make sentences.

1 [f] I'd like to visit
2 [ ] It's important to learn
3 [ ] I never send
4 [ ] When you have
5 [ ] I usually get
6 [ ] I often take

a about other people's cultures.
b a good idea, you must write it down.
c postcards to my friends.
d photos when I'm on holiday and put them on my Facebook page.
e a reply to my emails on the same day.
f a different country every year.

3 Match pictures A–F with words 1–6.

A

B

C
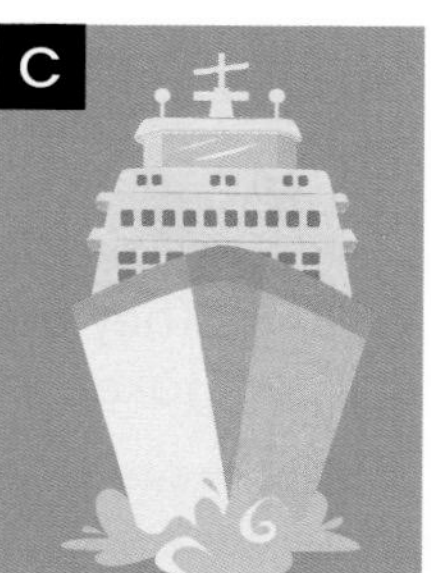
D

E

F

1 [C] cruise ship
2 [ ] stamp
3 [ ] gift
4 [ ] penguin
5 [ ] post office
6 [ ] post box

4 Choose the correct option.

1 I've got a good idea *of* / *for* a holiday.
2 Did you write *to* / *at* your English friend about his visit?
3 The film starts *with* / *by* two people on a beautiful beach.
4 When they were young, my parents travelled *around* / *along* Europe and America.
5 At school last week we learned *for* / *about* sea birds in the Antarctic.
6 My dad bought a picture *from* / *of* penguins from his holiday.

5 Complete the word puzzle. What's the hidden word?

	1 s	t	a	m	p			
		2						
3								
					4			
			5					
	6							
	7							

1 You put this on a letter when you go to the post office.
2 This is unusual and something you don't often see.
3 This is a mountain with fire inside.
4 You give this to someone on their birthday.
5 A holiday on a big boat.
6 People send you these when they answer your emails.
7 A person who finds new things.

The hidden word is: __________ .

6 **Read the video script. Underline any words or phrases you don't know and find their meaning in your dictionary.**

The Penguin Post Office

Antarctica is a very cold place for a holiday. It's 700 miles south of Argentina and Chile, but thousands of people come here every year. One of the most popular places to visit is Port Lockroy. They come here to see the Gentoo penguins and visit a very unusual British post office – the Penguin Post Office. There is a population of 3,000 penguins! The visitors take photos of some of them. They're very cute. Then they go inside. There's a gift shop and everything has got penguins on it. You can buy T-shirts, cups, toys and lots of other things. There are 18,000 visitors every summer. All the visitors want to tell their friends about the Penguin Post Office, so they write postcards. They write about the cold and the snow, and of course, they write about the penguins. Then they can post them in a real British post box. The postcards go all around the world. You have to put a stamp on a postcard. And what have the stamps got on them? Penguins, of course! The penguins are real stars!

9 Getting around

VOCABULARY
Transport | Travel

GRAMMAR
Present Continuous for future arrangements | *going to* for plans

READING
Day trip activities

LISTENING
The weather

SPEAKING
Directions

WRITING
An invitation

BBC CULTURE
Are there ghosts in the Underground?

EXAM TIME 3 > p. 122

9.1 VOCABULARY Transport and travel

I can talk about means of transport and travel.

1 Find eight means of transport in the word search. Look ↑, ↓, ↗ and ↘.

S	L	E	Q	N	M	T	E	E	P	D	A
D	J	P	U	T	M	A	S	E	D	E	H
O	T	J	N	D	X	X	A	S	K	J	E
H	I	U	D	C	O	I	V	I	S	I	D
W	F	A	E	E	N	P	B	U	S	Z	P
A	W	O	R	I	W	R	I	S	I	T	C
E	N	T	G	N	O	E	C	A	R	B	C
E	Z	R	R	T	O	I	Y	H	C	E	E
T	E	A	O	C	G	E	C	F	E	Z	L
A	I	M	U	I	A	A	L	S	R	A	T
E	O	E	N	E	O	P	E	A	X	M	M
N	N	G	D	C	X	D	Z	N	S	C	N

2 Look at the photos and complete the words.

1 b*us* st*ation*

2 u_ _ _ _ _ _ _ _ _

3 b_ _ _ l_ _ _

4 t_ _ _ _ s_ _ _ _ _ _

5 c_ _ p_ _ _

6 b_ _ s_ _ _

3 ●● **Complete the sentences with words from Exercise 2.**

1 The new *bus station* in the town centre is great. I use it a lot to visit my grandma. I can't afford trains.
2 Cycling in town is very dangerous. There aren't any ___________ and there are lots of accidents.
3 When we go to the cinema, you can leave your car in the big ___________ in the town centre.
4 There's a very small ___________ near our house, but it's very busy. People go to London for work from here every day. It's more expensive than the bus but it's faster!
5 I'm at the ___________ outside the library. I'm waiting for number 10. See you soon.
6 Oxford and Cambridge are the most famous ___________ in the UK.

4 ●● WORD FRIENDS **Choose the correct option.**

1 Are you travelling to the airport *in* / (*by*) car?
2 I learned to *drive* / *ride* a bike when I was five years old.
3 We waited *on* / *at* the bus stop for half an hour in the rain!
4 Can we go to the shops *on* / *by* foot? I need the exercise.
5 Can you help me get *on* / *at* the train please? These bags are very heavy.
6 Don't catch the number 11 bus. Wait *for* / *at* the number 15. It's quicker.
7 In our country you have to be seventeen years old to *ride* / *drive* a car.

5 ●● **Match 1–6 with a–f to make sentences.**

1 [c] I fell when I got
2 [ ] My brother's learning to drive
3 [ ] There was a long queue of people waiting
4 [ ] The concert was near our house, so we went
5 [ ] My dad's work is thirty kilometres away, so he always goes
6 [ ] Which bus is Charlie waiting

a for?
b on foot.
c off the train.
d a car.
e by train.
f at the bus stop.

6 ●● **Choose the correct answer.**

1 Get a ___ home after the cinema. It only costs £5.00.
   a car   b bike   (c) taxi
2 My sister's boyfriend rides a ___ . My mum thinks it's dangerous.
   a train   b coach   c motorbike
3 I'm meeting Tom at the bus ___ in five minutes.
   a park   b stop   c lane
4 How long did you have to wait ___ the bus?
   a for   b at   c to
5 The car ___ was full and we had to leave the car in the road.
   a station   b park   c stop
6 I usually ___ a bike to school.
   a drive   b go   c ride
7 Riding a bike isn't dangerous if there's a good bike ___ .
   a stop   b lane   c park

7 ●●● **Complete the email with one word in each gap.**

To: hello@jack.com

Hi Jack,

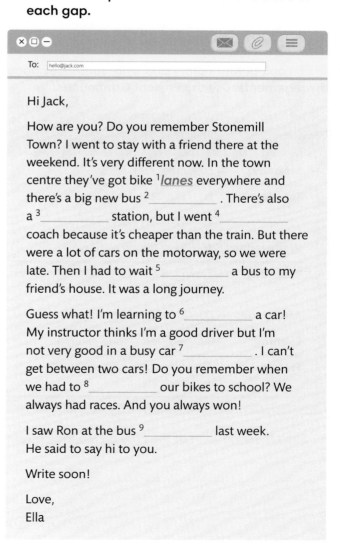

How are you? Do you remember Stonemill Town? I went to stay with a friend there at the weekend. It's very different now. In the town centre they've got bike [1]*lanes* everywhere and there's a big new bus [2]___________ . There's also a [3]___________ station, but I went [4]___________ coach because it's cheaper than the train. But there were a lot of cars on the motorway, so we were late. Then I had to wait [5]___________ a bus to my friend's house. It was a long journey.

Guess what! I'm learning to [6]___________ a car! My instructor thinks I'm a good driver but I'm not very good in a busy car [7]___________ . I can't get between two cars! Do you remember when we had to [8]___________ our bikes to school? We always had races. And you always won!

I saw Ron at the bus [9]___________ last week. He said to say hi to you.

Write soon!

Love,
Ella

9.2 GRAMMAR Present Continuous for future arrangements

I can use the Present Continuous to talk about future arrangements.

1 Complete the sentences with the Present Continuous form of the verbs in brackets.

1 I *'m swimming* (swim) in a competition on Saturday.
2 My friend ________ (fly) to France tomorrow.
3 We ________ (go) to London by train to see the concert next week.
4 Bob ________ (come) round this evening to play video games.
5 Stuart ________ (play) tennis every day next week.
6 I ________ (cook) dinner tonight for my parents.
7 Katy's mum and dad ________ (plan) a surprise party for her birthday next month.

2 Make the sentences in Exercise 1 negative.

1 *I'm not swimming in a competition on Saturday.*
2 ________
3 ________
4 ________
5 ________
6 ________
7 ________

3 Look at Kim's diary and write sentences about her arrangements. Use the Present Continuous.

uCalendar

WEEK 16

Monday:	4.30 – meet John at café
Tuesday:	5.30 – play tennis with Leo
	~~7.30 – go to art club~~
Wednesday:	8.45 – have dinner at Gary's
Thursday:	Morning, 8.15 – go to Salford Museum with class
Afternoon:	5.00 – arrive back at school
Evening:	~~Mum and Dad – go to cinema~~
Friday:	4.30: Mike – take part in hockey competition

1 *She's meeting John at the café on Monday afternoon.*
2 ________
3 ________
4 ________
5 ________
6 ________
7 ________
8 ________

4 Make questions in the Present Continuous. Then write short answers.

1 we / have / a test / on Monday / ?
A: *Are we having a test on Monday?*
B: Yes, ________.
2 Hannah / go / on holiday / soon / ?
A: ________
B: Yes, ________.
3 you / play / football / on Saturday / ?
A: ________
B: No, ________.
4 Mike and Sue / leave / next week / ?
A: ________
B: No, ________.
5 you / have / dinner with Jo / tonight / ?
A: ________
B: Yes, ________.

5 Complete the email with the Present Continuous form of the verbs below.

fly go (x2) have not go not stay play stay take

To: hello@jack.com

Hi Eva,

Have you got any plans for the weekend? [1]*Are you going* (you) to town with Nick tomorrow? There's a concert in the park in the afternoon and I think the Pink Elephants [2]________. Would you like to go? I [3]________ to the cinema with Jason in the evening because I have to pack. We [4]________ to New York from Gatwick Airport on Sunday! Jason [5]________ a barbecue for his birthday on Sunday afternoon. [6]________ (you)?

Do you know New York? It's my first visit. We [7]________ at a hotel – it's too expensive. We [8]________ with my dad's brother. He [9]________ us to a Broadway show next week. I can't wait!

Have a good weekend and speak soon!
Lily

9.3 READING and VOCABULARY | Day trip activities

I can find specific detail in a text and talk about day trip activities.

1 Match photos A–F with the activities below.

hiking sailing sightseeing skiing ~~sunbathing~~ surfing

A B C

1 *sunbathing* 2 ______ 3 ______

D E F

4 ______ 5 ______ 6 ______

2 Match the comments with the activities in Exercise 1.

1 'I've only got a small boat but I love being out on the water.' *sailing*
2 'My perfect holiday is lying on a beach.' ______
3 'When we were in Madrid, we saw some really interesting places.' ______
4 'Sometimes it's difficult to stand up, but the feeling is cool when you're on top of the waves!' ______
5 'Moving on snow is great!' ______
6 'My friend and I always put too many things in our bags and after a day our backs hurt.' ______

3 Read the descriptions of people looking for an activity to do on a day trip. Tick the things they like.

1 ☐ gardening
2 ☐ relaxing
3 ☐ walking
4 ☐ buying things
5 ☐ visiting old places
6 ☐ sunbathing
7 ☐ driving
8 ☐ sailing
9 ☐ cycling

1 ☐ John and Maya have two sons, who are eight and nine years old. They all love being outside. John and Maya are keen gardeners.

2 ☐ Brenda and her daughter Maggie enjoy relaxing when they're on holiday. They like the sea and the countryside. Brenda has a bad leg and can't walk a long way.

3 ☐ Tony and his French friend Charles are both interested in history and visiting old places. Tony loves driving his dad's old Rolls Royce. Charles prefers cycling through the countryside.

4 Read the adverts (A–D) for things to do on a day trip to a village called Beaulieu. Match them with the people in Exercise 3 (1–3). There is one extra advert.

A Are you coming to the Beaulieu area and looking for something interesting to do? You have to come to the Beaulieu Motor Museum. We have cars, bikes and motorbikes from 100 years ago. We also have the Donald Campbell's famous Bluebird boat. It broke the world speed record! Why not look round the Palace House as well? It's a wonderful old building with lovely gardens where you can have a picnic too.

B Beaulieu Village is an almost perfect English village and very beautiful. There are lots of small shops where you can buy local art and jewellery, and of course, there is also the famous Beaulieu Chocolate Shop. The smell in there is amazing! There's a tea shop for traditional cakes and a small garden centre with lots of flowers to look at or buy.

C Do you sometimes want life to be slower? Come on a boat trip along the Beaulieu river! Sit down and watch the English countryside go past. Feel the cool wind on your face. Then when the boat turns to come back, we stop at the lovely village Buckler's Hard for a coffee and a snack. You can go for a long walk around the Hard or just sit and enjoy the view in the café.

D If you're a fan of flowers and beautiful gardens, then you need to spend some time at Exbury Gardens. It's near Beaulieu and it's very popular with tourists. There's a small train that takes visitors round the gardens. The children love it! We also have a café and restaurant, and lots of activities for younger children. Come and see us!

9.4 GRAMMAR *going to* for plans

I can use *going to* to talk about future plans.

1 Complete the dialogues with the phrases below.

OUT of class

believe it or not lucky you tell me about it

1 A: That was a terrible test! I know I got everything wrong!
B: ______________!
2 A: Are you coming out with us tonight?
B: No! ______________, I'm going to do my English homework!
3 A: I got £200 for my birthday!
B: ______________!

2 ● Look at the pictures and write sentences. Use the correct form of *going to* and the phrases below.

buy some books online ~~chat to my friends~~
play with my brother relax in the garden
tidy my bedroom wash my hair

A

1 *I'm going to chat to my friends.*

B

2 ______________

C

3 ______________

D

4 ______________

E

5 ______________

F

6 ______________

3 ●● Order the words to make sentences.

1 going / is / Tommy / emails / dinner / to / write / some / after
Tommy's going to write some emails after dinner.
2 not / we / the / in / going / long / to / are / stay / for / park
____
3 get / Cathy and Mark / to / soon / going / married / are / ?
____
4 lot / I'm / going / not / a / the / at / restaurant / to / eat
____
5 drink / isn't / Lyn / coffee / to / for / going / month / a
____
6 going / they / book / centre / to / in / are / city / hotel / the / a / ?
____

4 ●●● Complete the dialogue with the correct form of *going to* and the verbs below.

come ~~do~~ drive go (x2) look
not stay show visit (x2)

Jade: So, what [1]*are you going to do* (you) when your American friend comes to stay?
Paul: Oh, I've got lots of plans. We [2]______________ here in Barchester all the time! We [3]______________ my cousins in Wales for a few days.
Jade: Wonderful! [4]______________ (you) up Mount Snowdon?
Paul: No, we aren't - that's hard work! We [5]______________ round the countryside in my cousins' car because it's very beautiful in North Wales. So, we [6]______________ at Snowdon, but that's it!
Jade: And then?
Paul: OK, after Wales I [7]______________ him some interesting places in London. We [8]______________ to some museums, I think. How about you? [9]______________ (your German friend) this summer?
Jade: No. I [10]______________ her this year but I don't know the dates yet.

I can identify specific detail in conversations and talk about the weather.

1 Look at the pictures and complete the crossword.

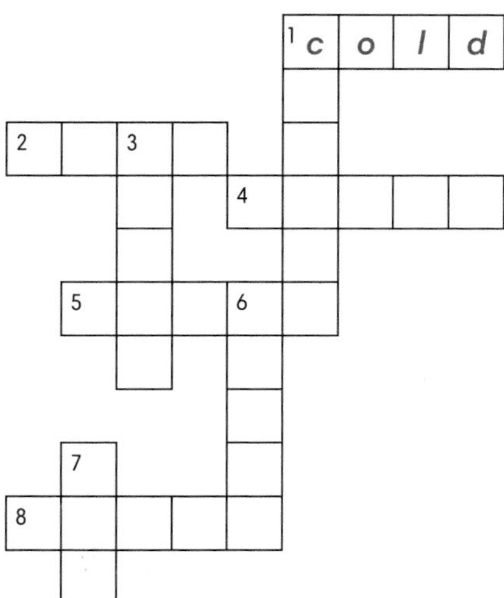

Across

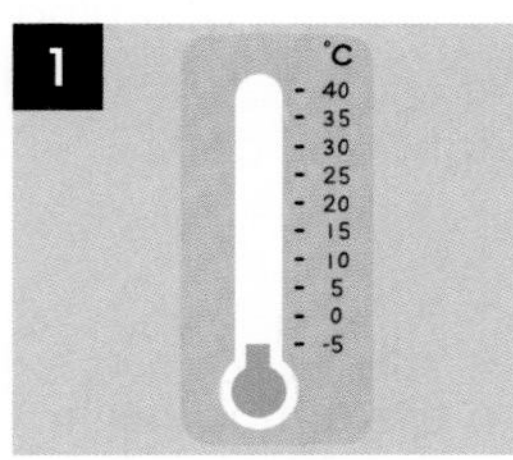

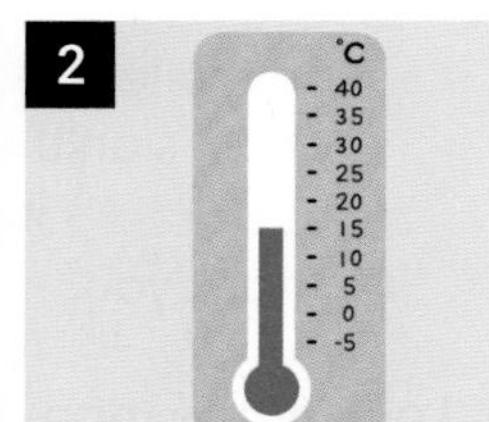

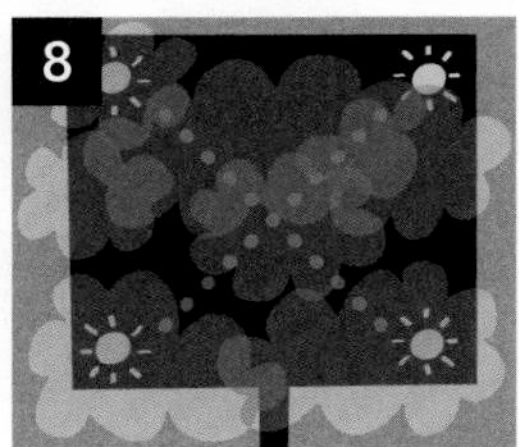

Down

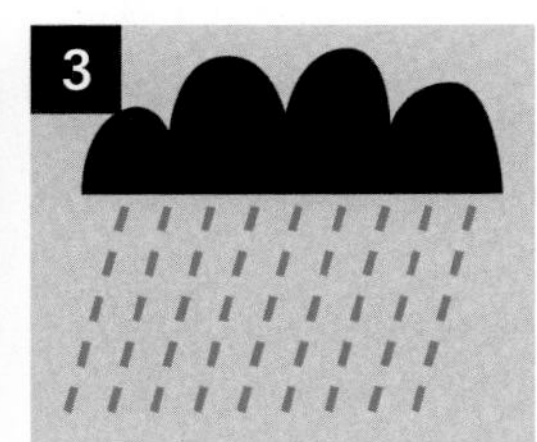

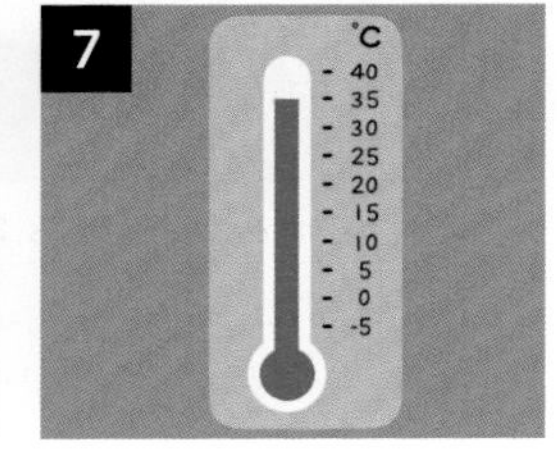

2 Complete the sentences with words from Exercise 1.

1 The children can't get to school because it's *snowy* and the cars can't drive down the roads.
2 It's often very ________ in January and we need our umbrellas a lot.
3 I don't like the weather when it's very hot or very cold. ________ is nice!
4 It's ________ in the garden – put some cream on your face.
5 It's dangerous to drive when it's very ________ because you can't see much. You need special lights on the car.
6 It was so ________ yesterday that some trees in the garden fell down.
7 There isn't much sun today because it's quite ________ .
8 You need a hat and gloves – it's very ________ outside.
9 It's really ________ in the south of Spain in the summer – sometimes even forty degrees.

3 18 Listen and match pictures A–C with situations 1–3.

4 18 Listen again. Choose the correct answer.

1 The girl can't go to
 a school. b a party. c the shops.
2 The weather at the moment is
 a cloudy. b rainy. c sunny.
3 Which picture shows the weather yesterday morning?

I can ask for and give directions.

1 Complete the dialogues with the phrases below. OUT of class

Good thinking! Just a sec!

1 A: Let's go for a bike ride.
B: ______ The weather's perfect for it – it's sunny but not too hot.

2 A: Let's go for a bike ride.
B: ______ I have to finish this email.

2 Match questions 1–3 with answers a–c.

1 [ ] Excuse me. Where is the bank?
2 [ ] Is there a bank near here?
3 [ ] How do I get to the bank?

a Take the first turning on the right. Go straight on. You can't miss it.
b Yes, there's one in Green Street.
c It's opposite the cinema at the end of the road.

3 Order the words to give directions.

1 straight / go / on
Go straight on.
2 end / to / road / of / the / go / the
______
3 the / past / café / go
______
4 left / crossroads / turn / the / at
______
5 second / on / take / right / the / turning / the
______
6 the / next / bank / to / it's
______
7 the / it's / on / right
______
8 opposite / it's / station / the
______

4 Complete the dialogues with one word in each gap.

1 A: Excuse me. Where's the [a]?
B: It's not far. Go to the ______ of the High Street and turn right. Go ______ on and it's on ______ left.
A: Thanks!

2 A: Excuse me. Is there a [b] ______ here?
B: Yes. There's one in Harvest Road. ______ straight on and turn left ______ the traffic lights. It's on the left. It's opposite a big garage.
A: Thank you very much.

3 A: Excuse me. How do I ______ to the new [c]?
B: OK. ______ the second turning on the left. Go ______ the hotel and it's on the right. You can't ______ it.
A: Thank you.

5 Look at the map and the dialogues in Exercise 4. Where do the people want to go? Write the words for [a]–[c].

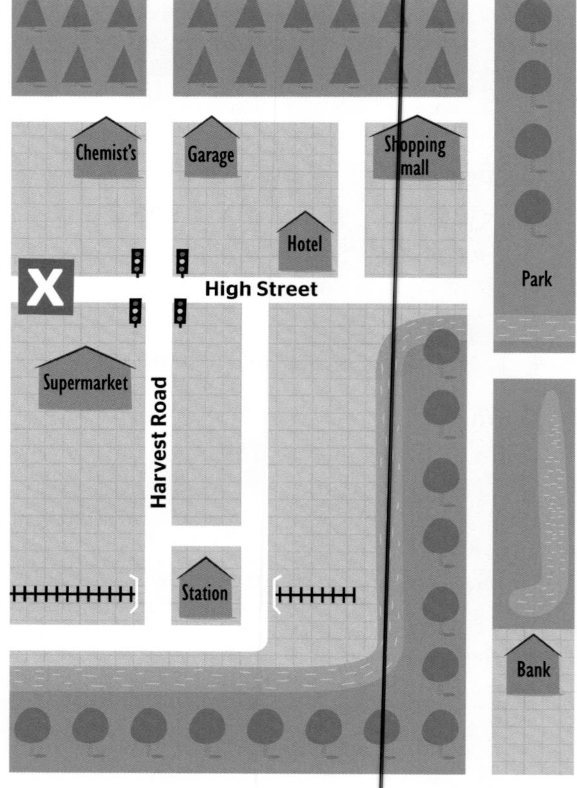

a ______
b ______
c ______

9.7 WRITING An invitation

I can write an invitation email.

1 Complete the email with one word in each gap.

To: hello@dave.com

[1]*Hi* Dave,

[2] ________ are you? I hope your swimming competition was good last Saturday. Did you win? Did you [3] ________ the news? My sister Wendy is [4] ________ to get married! She's marrying Jake. She met him at university. The wedding's next year.

My parents are planning a party to [5] ________ their engagement. They're going to [6] ________ lots of Wendy and Jake's friends. I [7] ________ invite some friends too, so I'd [8] ________ to invite you! I'm also going to invite Mandy and Sasha. It's [9] ________ Saturday 11 July [10] ________ our house. It's going to start [11] ________ 7.30. Can you [12] ________ ? I [13] ________ so.

Write [14] ________ soon.

Love,
Sara

2 Read the email again. Answer the questions.

1 Who wrote the email?
Sara
2 What did Dave do last weekend?
3 What is the news?
4 Where did Wendy and Jake meet?
5 Who is planning the party?
6 When is the party?
7 Where is the party?
8 What time is the party?
9 Who else is coming to the party?

3 Order the words to make sentences for greeting, giving news, inviting and making arrangements.

1 a / having / we're / barbecue
We're having a barbecue.
2 are / you / how / ?
3 on / my / birthday / Sunday / it's
4 to / invite / I'd / you / like / to / party / my
5 come / you / can / ?
6 news / the / hear / did / you / ?
7 at / starts / the / 7.30 / party
8 my / passed / I / exams
9 the / outside / meet / let's / café

4 You are planning a surprise birthday party for your friend Gemma. You are going to email another friend to invite them. Make some notes.

- *person you are inviting*
- *reason for the party*
- *type of party*
- *date, time and place of the party*
- *any other information?*

5 Write your email. Remember to do these things.

- Use Sara's email to help you.
- Use the right phrases for news, invitations and arrangements.
- Start and end your email with appropriate phrases.

9.8 SELF-ASSESSMENT

For each learning objective, tick (✓) the box that best matches your ability.

☺☺ = I understand and can help a friend.

☺ = I understand and can do it by myself.

☹ = I understand but have some questions.

☹☹ = I do not understand.

		☺☺	☺	☹	☹☹	Need help?	Now try ...
9.1	Vocabulary					Students' Book pp. 106–107 Workbook pp. 102–103	Ex. 1–4, p. 111
9.2	Grammar					Students' Book p. 108 Workbook p. 104	Ex. 5–6, p. 111
9.3	Reading					Students' Book p. 109 Workbook p. 105	
9.4	Grammar					Students' Book p. 110 Workbook p. 106	Ex. 5–6, p. 111
9.5	Listening					Students' Book p. 111 Workbook p. 107	
9.6	Speaking					Students' Book p. 112 Workbook p. 108	Ex. 7, p. 111
9.7	Writing					Students' Book p. 113 Workbook p. 109	

9.1 I can talk about means of transport and travel.
9.2 I can use the Present Continuous to talk about future arrangements.
9.3 I can find specific detail in a text and talk about day trip activities.
9.4 I can use *going to* to talk about future plans.
9.5 I can identify specific detail in conversations and talk about the weather.
9.6 I can ask for and give directions.
9.7 I can write an invitation email.

What can you remember from this unit?

New words I learned (the words you most want to remember from this unit)	**Expressions and phrases I liked** (any expressions or phrases you think sound nice, useful or funny)	**English I heard or read outside class** (e.g. from websites, books, adverts, films, music)

9.9 SELF-CHECK

Vocabulary

1 Complete the words.

1 A big place where people can leave their cars: **c**_ _ **p**_ _ _
2 This means of transport goes under houses and roads: **u**_ _ _ _ _ _ _ _ _ _ _
3 This is like a bicycle but it goes very fast and you don't need to pedal: **m**_ _ _ _ _ _ _ _
4 You wait here for a bus: **b**_ _ **s**_ _ _
5 People on bikes use this when they're cycling in towns: **b**_ _ _ **l**_ _ _
6 This is like a bus but people use it for longer journeys: **c**_ _ _ _

2 Complete the sentences with prepositions.

1 Go to London ______ train. It's faster.
2 I'm waiting ______ the 59 bus.
3 The taxi driver opened the door and we all got ______ the taxi.
4 Don't forget: get ______ the train at Lyndhurst.
5 We went to the bus station ______ foot because it's very near our house.

3 Match activities 1–5 with places a–e.

1 ☐ skiing
2 ☐ sunbathing
3 ☐ hiking
4 ☐ sightseeing
5 ☐ surfing

a on the water
b on the snow
c through the mountains
d on the beach
e in the city

4 Read the comments. What weather conditions are they talking about?

1 'We're going to get wet!' ______________
2 'The garden is so quiet and white.' ______________
3 'You mustn't drive. You can't see anything outside!' ______________
4 'Great weather for sunbathing.' ______________
5 'The tops of the tress are moving!' ______________

Grammar

5 Read Mike's notes and write sentences about his arrangements. Use the Present Continuous.

1 Meet Jack: train station – 8.30
2 Have History test: Friday morning
3 Swim in competition: Saturday afternoon
4 Go to art club: today – 4.15
5 Catch 9.15 train to London tomorrow morning
6 Have barbecue : Sunday afternoon – 2.30

1 He's ______________________________.
2 He's ______________________________.
3 He's ______________________________.
4 He ______________________________.
5 He ______________________________.
6 He ______________________________.

6 Complete the sentences with the correct form of *going to* and the verbs below.

buy call correct go visit work

1 I ______________ to bed early tonight because I'm tired.
2 Mum ______________ her friend Lindsay later this evening on her new smartphone.
3 My sister ______________ her friend in Germany next summer.
4 I ______________ harder at school next year!
5 Jan and Eva ______________ a new car next year.
6 Our teacher ______________ our tests before Friday.

Speaking language practice

7 Choose the correct option.

1 A: Excuse me. [1]*Where* / *There* is the station?
B: Go to the [2]*far* / *end* of the road and [3]*on* / *turn* right. It's [4]*in* / *on* the left.

2 A: Excuse me. Is [5]*it* / *there* a supermarket near here?
B: Yes. Go [6]*straight* / *past* the bank and [7]*take* / *turn* the first turning on the right. It's [8]*opposite* / *next* to the Hotel Excelsior. It's not [9]*far* / *long*.

3 A: Excuse me. How do I [10]*get* / *find* to the river?
B: Turn right [11]*at* / *next* the traffic lights. Go [12]*left* / *straight* on and you can't [13]*find* / *miss* it!

1 Match pictures A–E with words 1–5.

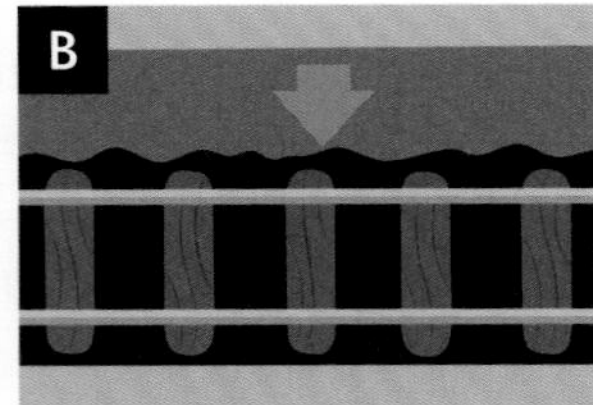
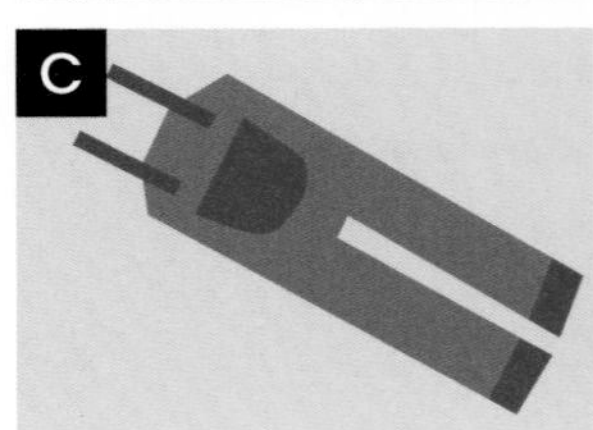

1 [B] track
2 [ ] ghost
3 [ ] overalls
4 [ ] tube
5 [ ] electrician

2 Complete the words in the sentences.

1 I watched a very sc*ary* film yesterday and I couldn't sleep!
2 You must be well-d_ _ _s_d for an interview.
3 This Maths problem isn't easy – it's very c_m_ _ _c_ _ _d.
4 The road doesn't turn. It goes s_ _ _ _ _ _t for a kilometre.
5 David is c_nf_ _ _n_ when he does tests because he knows lots of things.
6 It's hard for b_ _ _d people to walk across busy roads.

3 Complete the sentences with *going to* and the verbs below.

design drive fall ~~leave~~ not take scream touch

1 We *'re going to leave* school early today.
2 Be careful! You ______________ !
3 He ______________ public transport to Leeds. He ______________ in his dad's car.
4 Oh no! It's a snake. I ______________ !
5 We ______________ a special poster for the show.
6 I ______________ the painting. I hope it's dry!

4 Match A–E in the picture with words 1–5.

1 [D] platform
2 [ ] sign
3 [ ] map
4 [ ] underground train
5 [ ] escalator

5 Match 1–5 with a–e to make sentences.

1 [c] He's waiting
2 [ ] He's going
3 [ ] They're looking
4 [ ] She's trying
5 [ ] She can't see

a a new system.
b the sign.
c on the platform.
d at a map.
e up the escalator.

6 Complete the crossword with words from this page.

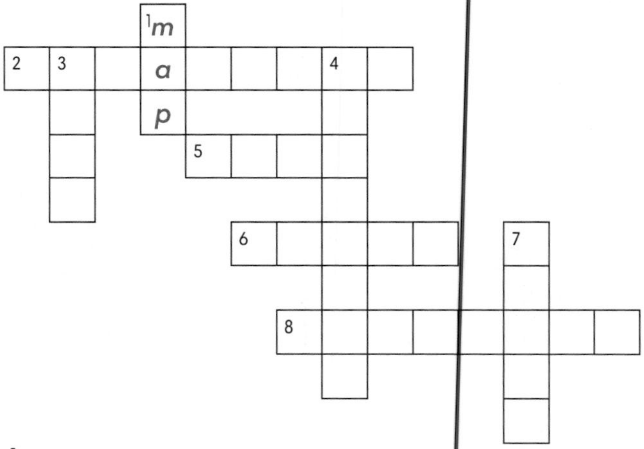

(Crossword grid: 1 down begins *m*, *a*, *p*.)

Across
2 The stairs move on this.
5 Another name for the London Underground.
6 The train goes along this.
8 You wait for a train on this.

Down
1 It helps you find the way.
3 You can look at this for information.
4 People wear these when they are working.
7 You think you can see this, but it isn't real.

7 **Read the video script. Underline any words or phrases you don't know and find their meaning in your dictionary.**

Travelling on the tube

Underground stations are sometimes difficult to use. There are lots of platforms and escalators. One station sometimes has lots of different lines. Usually there are signs and maps to help us. But imagine that you're blind – you can't see. It's very difficult to find your way. Lauren can't see very well. When she gets off a train, she doesn't know where to go. But today a voice in her ear tells her, 'Turn right.' Today Lauren is testing some new technology. It's to help people find their way on the London Underground. Lauren has a special smartphone. 'The up escalator is on your right.' Lauren is happy. Usually a journey on the Underground is very scary. She can't see the maps and she can't read the signs. Today she's more confident. Tom is also testing the technology. 'Go up the escalator and turn left.' He thinks it's going to help a lot of people. The technology can also help tourists and people who can't read or understand English. Lauren and her friends helped to design the new system. It's the end of the journey and the end of the test. It works. A great success!

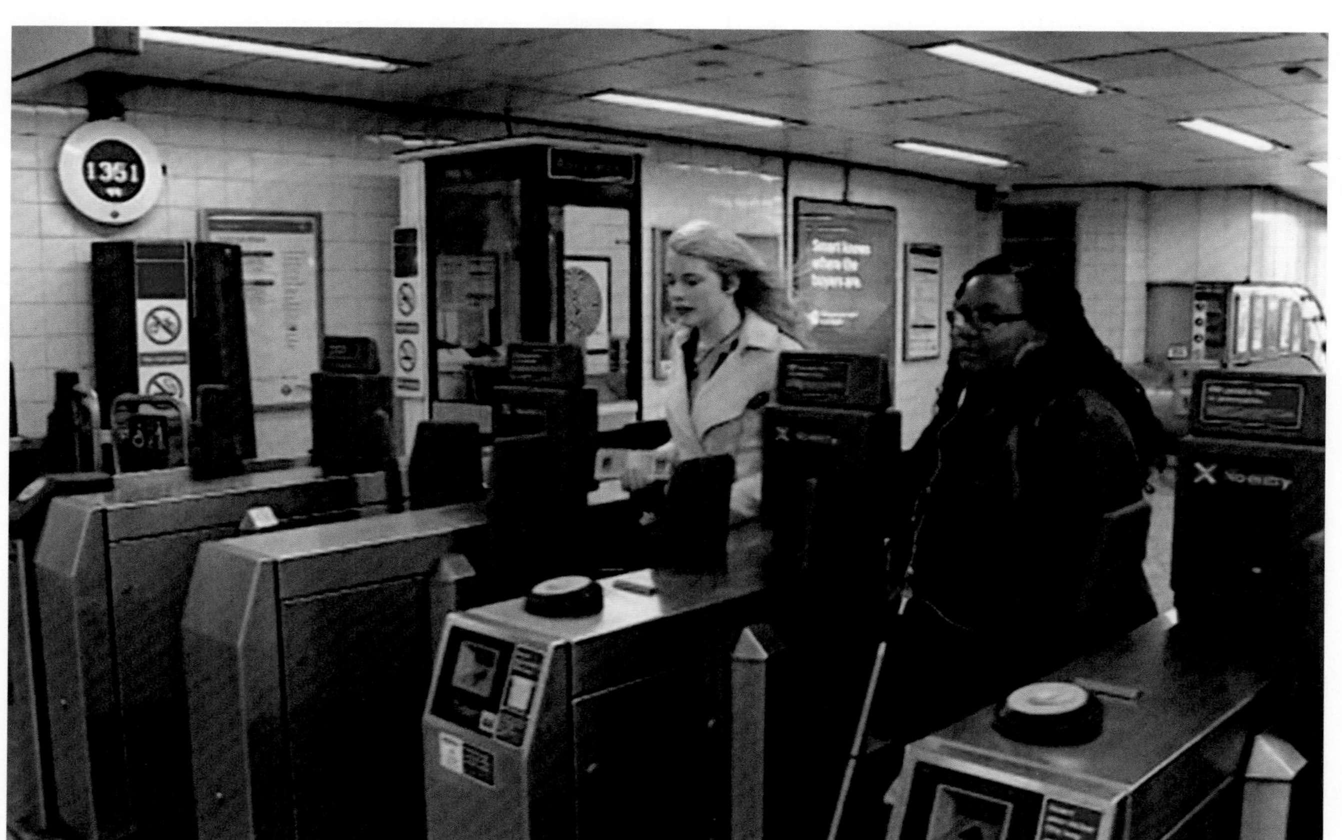

1 Match sentences 1–6 with notices A–H.

Tip: You won't always see the same words in the notices and the sentences.

1 [E] You can't eat here today.
2 [ ] Children can watch this.
3 [ ] You can't text people in here.
4 [ ] Phone for information.
5 [ ] People don't eat meat here.
6 [ ] You can't wear some clothes to this.

A
School dinner party
No jeans or trainers, please.

B
NO PHONES
IN THE CLASSROOM

C
Jack's Cat
A film for all the family

D
Buy Kate Best's new book
about a very interesting family.

E
Park Restaurant
Closed for two weeks
Opens 2 December

F
Care Dog's Home
You can find a new pet here.

G
New Vegetarian Café
Great menu! Come and try!

H
DOG WALKING
07654982431

2 Read the sentences about a friend's family. Choose the best word (A, B or C) for each gap.

Tip: You need to think about the grammar and the meaning of the words to fit the sentences.

1 My friend's ___ is a very tall man.
A auntie B daughter (C) husband
2 He wears ___ clothes to work.
A happy B smart C strong
3 He ___ football on Saturdays.
A plays B goes C makes
4 They've ___ a young son called Harry.
A get B have C got
5 He wakes ___ every morning at 5.30!
A to B up C for
6 He likes ___ fingers for dinner.
A chicken B potato C fish

3 **Complete the conversations.**

A Yes, I am.

Is Marie English?

B Yes, she is.

C Yes, she does.

Tip: Remember that these are short dialogues, so you need a reply to the first comment or question.

1 Is Marie English?
  A Yes, I am.
  (B) Yes, she is.
  C Yes, she does.
2 Where do you live?
  A I want to live here.
  B In London.
  C No, I don't live here.
3 How many dogs have you got?
  A Three.
  B Two cats.
  C I've got a dog.
4 Can you come to the party?
  A It's a pity.
  B Yes, we are, thank you.
  C Sorry, I can't.
5 How are you?
  A Nice to meet you.
  B Fine, thanks.
  C Hi there.
6 Anything else?
  A Some ketchup, please.
  B It's delicious.
  C Here you are.

4 **Complete the telephone conversation between two friends. Match gaps 1–6 with sentences A–H.**

Tip: Read the whole dialogue first so that you understand the general meaning.

A: Hi, Liam. It's Louise.
B: 1 *B*
A: Fine, thanks. And you?
B: 2 ___
A: Have you got karate tonight?
B: 3 ___
A: Do you want to come here and listen to some music?
B: 4 ___
A: About 6.00. Mum says, 'Can you stay for dinner?'
B: 5 ___
A: Yeah! And today it's your favourite: fish and chips!
B: 6 ___
A: See you.

A Yes, I finish very late.
B Oh hi! How are you?
C Yes, please! Your mum's a great cook!
D Good idea! After our homework! What time?
E Cool! I love them!
F Can I help you?
G No, that's on Thursday.
H I'm OK, thanks, but I've got lots of homework.

5 **Read Cara's email to a new friend. Mark the sentences A (right), B (wrong) or C (doesn't say).**

Tip: Read the complete text first so that you know which part to look at for the answer. Then read that part again.

Hi Karen!

I want to tell you that I'm very happy to write to you. I can practise my English! And I get a new friend in a different country.

OK, about me. In my family there's me, my mum and my dad. My best friend, Robby, has got four brothers and two sisters. It's always busy in his house! My house is very quiet. I've got a dog and a cat. I want a pony but my mum says no!

At school I have a favourite teacher. Her name is Miss Jones and she teaches English. We study English on Mondays and Wednesdays. I also learn French, but I learn that on Friday evening at a French club. I usually stay at home in the evening and I often chat with my friends online. I like reading and cooking. My favourite meal is spaghetti and cheese. I hope you can come and stay with me next year. I can cook some lovely Italian food for you.

Write soon. Have you got a big family? What are your hobbies? It's good to have an English friend!

Bye for now,
Cara

1 Cara is English.
A Right **(B)** Wrong C Doesn't say
2 She's got a big family.
A Right B Wrong C Doesn't say
3 She studies with Robby.
A Right B Wrong C Doesn't say
4 She's got two pets.
A Right B Wrong C Doesn't say
5 Her favourite lesson is English.
A Right B Wrong C Doesn't say
6 She learns English and French at school.
A Right B Wrong C Doesn't say
7 She doesn't usually go out with her friends in the evening.
A Right B Wrong C Doesn't say
8 She can cook.
A Right B Wrong C Doesn't say

6 **Read the advertisement for a dog walker. Choose the best word (A, B or C) for each gap.**

Tip: The word must fit the grammar or meaning of the words around the gap. Are you looking for a verb, a preposition, a pronoun or is it an adjective or a noun?

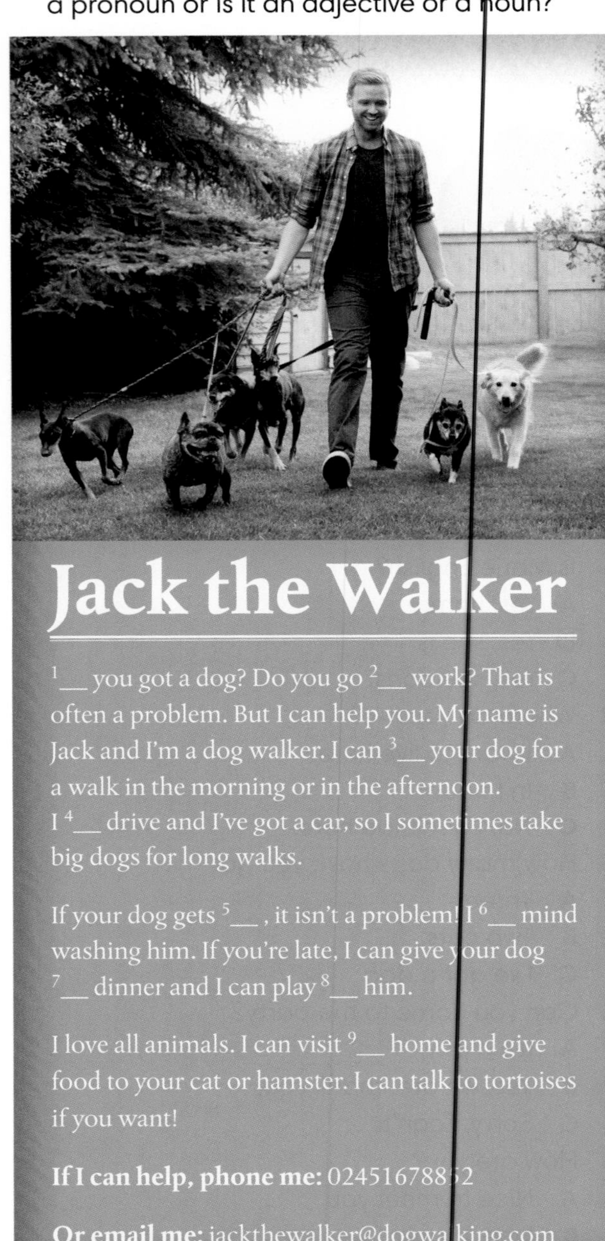
Jack the Walker
[1]__ you got a dog? Do you go [2]__ work? That is often a problem. But I can help you. My name is Jack and I'm a dog walker. I can [3]__ your dog for a walk in the morning or in the afternoon. I [4]__ drive and I've got a car, so I sometimes take big dogs for long walks.
If your dog gets [5]__, it isn't a problem! I [6]__ mind washing him. If you're late, I can give your dog [7]__ dinner and I can play [8]__ him.
I love all animals. I can visit [9]__ home and give food to your cat or hamster. I can talk to tortoises if you want!
If I can help, phone me: 024516788[illegible]2
Or email me: jackthewalker@dogwalking.com

	A	B	C
1	A Do	**(B)** Have	C Are
2	A to	B at	C for
3	A have	B go	C take
4	A don't	B does	C can
5	A dirty	B funny	C thirsty
6	A can't	B am not	C don't
7	A any	B many	C some
8	A on	B with	C to
9	A you	B your	C yours

7 **Read the descriptions of some words about clothes. What is the word for each one? The first letter is already there.**

Tip: Count the number of letters, to check you have the right word.

1 You wear these on your feet. **s***h o e s*
2 You put this on your head. **h**_ _
3 You wear this when you exercise. **t**_ _ _ _ _ _ _
4 Girls can wear this but not boys. **d**_ _ _ _
5 You wear these when it's hot. **s**_ _ _ _ _
6 You wear these over your eyes in the sun. **s**_ _ _ _ _ _ _ _ _

8 **Complete the email. Write ONE word for each gap.**

Tip: When you've finished, read the email again with your words and see if it makes sense.

To: ricky@fastmessage.com

Hi Ricky,

How [1]*are* you? [2]________ you like your new school? Have you [3]________ a lot of new friends?

I'm in Scotland now [4]________ my family. My granny [5]________ Scottish. She comes [6]________ Edinburgh. Today is [7]________ birthday and [8]________ is a big family party on Sunday.

It's very quiet here. There aren't many houses or people. But there are [9]________ of dogs and ponies! The food [10]________ very good here. I eat too [11]________ every day!

Write soon!
Amanda

9 **Read the advert and the email. Complete Meg's notes.**

Tip: Be careful when copying the spelling of names.

Cookery competition for television!
Bake a cake and be on television!
Come and watch on 2 November
at Brownswood School.
10.30–12.30 and 2.30–4.30

From: Gina;
To: Meg;

My sister's in the competition on Saturday. Do you want to come and watch? She's in the afternoon competition. We can leave here at 2.00. Dad can drive us there. Bring your camera – we can take some good photos!

Meg's notes

What competition? [1]*cookery*
Date: [2]
Place: [3]
Time to go: [4]
Go by: [5]
Take: [6]

10 **Read the email from your friend Jason.**

Tip: Plan your email and include answers to all the questions.

From: Jason;
To:

It's Friday! What do you want to do tomorrow? Do you want to go shopping? Perhaps the cinema or a walk with the dogs? Then maybe a snack at the café?

Write an email to Jason and answer the questions. Write 25–35 words.

1 Match sentences 1–6 with notices A–H.

Tip: The sentence you choose should have exactly the same meaning as the notice.

1 [H] You can't play a sport here today.
2 [ ] You can watch a sports match here.
3 [ ] Phone this number if you lost something.
4 [ ] Get an instrument here.
5 [ ] This class needs to go to a different room.
6 [ ] Check sports results here.

A

All football scores on
saturdaysports.com

B

Concert practice
7.30–9.00., main hall

C

Laptop found
Call me: 0976345210

D
Guitar club
Beginners: Mondays and Thursdays

E

Café Rouge
Football World Cup on TV
France v England: 2.00 today

F
3A Maths today – go to R15

G
Mann's Music
Cheap saxophones and flutes this week only!

H
Table-tennis table broken
New one on Monday

2 Read the sentences about a new leisure centre. Choose the best word (A, B or C) for each gap.

Tip: Think about the words that come before and after the gaps. This can help you choose the right word.

1 Last Saturday a new leisure centre ___ in Tom's town.
A was (B) opened C starts
2 He ___ there with his friend James.
A were B went C go
3 They're ___ on judo and swimming.
A interested B like C keen
4 James is a very ___ swimmer.
A talented B long C best
5 He often ___ cups in competitions.
A scores B plays C wins
6 The centre was ___ busy but they had great fun.
A enough B very C a lot

3 **Complete the conversations.**

A That's a
great idea!
B Of course.
C Yes, I can.

Tip: Try to imagine a possible reply before you look at the choices.

1 Can I make a suggestion?
   A That's a great idea!
   Ⓑ Of course.
   C Yes, I can.
2 I won the competition.
   A When is it on?
   B Poor you!
   C Well done!
3 Why don't we go out?
   A What about going out?
   B That's a great idea!
   C No, I prefer to go out.
4 Were you at home last night?
   A I'm watching TV.
   B I can't come out.
   C I went to the gym.
5 What's wrong?
   A I lost the match.
   B I wasn't into sport.
   C It was a wonderful game.
6 Can you help me, please?
   A Yes, no problem.
   B Sorry, I need it.
   C No, I'm not.

4 **Complete the telephone conversation between two friends. Match gaps 1–6 with sentences A–H.**

Tip: There will be clues in the sentences before or after the gap – sometimes in both.

A: Hi, Tim. How was the concert?
B: [1] *H*
A: Were there a lot of people?
B: [2] ___
A: Wow! And the room isn't very big.
B: [3] ___
A: That's good. Was your solo OK?
B: [4] ___
A: You're a great cello player! I want to come tonight. Are there any tickets?
B: [5] ___
A: After the concert let's go out for a meal.
B: [6] ___
A: Oh yes! I'm really into that food. See you tonight.

A No, you're right. Some people stood up! But they really liked the music.
B Oh yes, lots. It's only £5.
C Where do you want to go?
D Yes, there was a big audience – 200 people!
E Yes, thanks. I was nervous but I was alright.
F We finished at 9.30.
G That's a good idea. Why don't we go to the new vegetarian restaurant?
H It was good, thanks.

5 Read Marty's blog post about sports. Mark the sentences A (right), B (wrong) or C (doesn't say).

Tip: Sometimes an option is mentioned or suggested in the text but it isn't clearly right or wrong. Then it's probably *Doesn't say.*

Marty's job

I'm really into sport. My parents took me to tennis lessons when I was very young. I was only three years old! Then, two years later, I started judo and I really enjoyed it. When I was eleven, I got a brilliant new bicycle for my birthday and I started cycling. I was good and I was in the national team. I won lots of medals for my country. My big brother also loves sport – he's a professional football player. He gets a lot of money. It's great if your hobby can be your job.

I wanted to be a professional cyclist but I broke my leg when I was thirteen. Now I can't do a lot of sport. It made me very sad. But I found a new job with sport! Now I write about sport for a website. I love it. Every weekend I go to matches and tournaments. Then I write about them. Of course, I'm still a student and I can't write every day. When I'm eighteen, I want to go to university and learn to be a better writer. Then I can be a professional and get lots of money from sport, like my big brother!

1 Marty's parents are tennis players.
A Right B Wrong (C) Doesn't say
2 He did two sports when he was very young.
A Right B Wrong C Doesn't say
3 He started one sport because of a present.
A Right B Wrong C Doesn't say
4 He was a world cycling champion.
A Right B Wrong C Doesn't say
5 Marty's brother does the same sport as Marty.
A Right B Wrong C Doesn't say
6 Marty is thirteen.
A Right B Wrong C Doesn't say
7 Marty writes about his brother's matches.
A Right B Wrong C Doesn't say
8 Marty is studying at university.
A Right B Wrong C Doesn't say

6 Read the article about the Brit School. Choose the best word (A, B or C) for each gap.

Tip: Remember that two of the options are close to the correct answer but don't fit exactly.

The Brit School

Do you [1]___ about the Brit School? It's one of the [2]___ famous schools in the UK. It isn't famous for [3]___ exam results and you don't study subjects like Maths and Science there. It's a school for actors, singers, musicians, dancers and artists. I'm sure you know [4]___ of its old students. Do you like Adele's or Amy Winehouse's music? They went [5]___ the Brit School!

The school started [6]___ 1991. It's in Croydon, London. In 1991 it was small but now it's bigger [7]___ it was then. It's also unusual because students don't [8]___ to pay for lessons there. It's free.

Every year there are the famous Brit Awards. People [9]___ lots of countries watch them on television. Money from these awards helps the students.

	A	B	C
1	A understand	B read	(C) know
2	A more	B most	C much
3	A its	B his	C their
4	A any	B enough	C some
5	A at	B to	C by
6	A on	B of	C in
7	A from	B of	C than
8	A have	B got	C want
9	A of	B on	C from

7 **Read the descriptions of some words about music. What is the word for each one? The first letter is already there.**

Tip: Words like *this*, *these*, *where*, etc. can help you decide what sort of word you need.

1 This is a musical instrument. **p***iano*
2 It's a kind of music. **c**_ _ _ _ _ _ _ _
3 This is a group of people who play instruments. **o**_ _ _ _ _ _ _ _
4 You wear these to listen to music. **h**_ _ _ _ _ _ _ _ _
5 People read this before they go to a concert. **r**_ _ _ _ _
6 This is the group of people who watch a concert. **a**_ _ _ _ _ _ _

8 **Complete the email. Write ONE word for each gap.**

Tip: Sometimes more than one word seems to fit but look carefully at the word before and after - only one will be right.

To: diana@fastmessage.com

Hi Diana,

We had a test in Geography today and it [1]*was* terrible! I revised [2]________ it a lot last night but the questions were about different things! And there were too [3]________ questions – there wasn't [4]________ time to do them all! It was worse [5]________ my last test and I got very bad marks for that one! There were [6]________ of hard questions about countries and towns. I hope your day was [7]________ than mine!

I think you [8]________ to see the Big Four concert [9]________ weekend. Was it good? I wanted [10]________ go but there weren't [11]______ tickets.

Phone me and tell me about it!
Sue

9 **Read the advert and the email. Complete Blake's notes.**

Tip: The texts will have some information that you do not need. Read the questions carefully, to make sure you know what information you are looking for.

Maths lessons
Is Maths hard for you?
Have you got exams soon? I can help!
Phone me: 078 967 8674 231
Or email me: ben@mathsteacher.com

From: Mark;
To: Blake;

Hey! I saw this and thought about you! I know this teacher, Anne Jones – she's really good. She taught my sister and she passed her exams! Anne can come to your home after school or you can go to her house in Manchester Road. She isn't expensive – £10, and that's for an hour and a half. I think she can help you. I know you're worried. Phone her tonight!

Blake's notes
Advert for: [1]*Maths teacher*
Name: [2]________
Address: [3]________
How long is a lesson? [4]________
Cost: [5]________
Email: [6]________

10 **Read the email from your friend Terry.**

Tip: Try to give a reason for some of your answers to the questions with *because*.

From: Terry;
To:

It's good you can come here this evening. Let's watch a concert online. Which band do you want to see? What time can you come round? Do you want to eat here or go out before?

Write an email to Terry and answer the questions. Write 25–35 words.

1 Match sentences 1–6 with notices A–H.

Tip: Try to guess where you might see the notices. This can help you match the explanations.

1 [H] You can't park in this place.
2 [ ] You can have a cheap holiday here.
3 [ ] People aren't travelling by train from here today.
4 [ ] You have to pay to visit this place.
5 [ ] You mustn't go in the water.
6 [ ] You have to write something on this.

A Fareham Station closed all day. Opens tomorrow, 6.30

B Changes to bus timetable: Monday–Saturday only from this stop

C School skiing holiday
Names below, please – before Friday

D PALACE HOUSE
ALL TICKETS £10.00

E Avon Hotel
3 nights for price of 2 in November!

F NO DOGS ON BEACH

G

H NO CARS IN ROAD

2 Read the sentences about a holiday. Choose the best word (A, B or C) for each gap.

Tip: If you can't decide on the right answer, take out the ones you think are wrong and choose the one that remains.

1 My friend's family ___ me on holiday last month.
A had B went (C) took

2 We went ___ car to a town near the sea.
A in B on C by

3 The ___ was very hot and sunny.
A weather B sun C time

4 We sunbathed on the beach ___ day.
A often B usually C every

5 I bought some ___ and sent them to my family.
A photos B letters C postcards

6 We arrived home ___ night.
A last B before C ago

3 **Complete the conversations.**

Mr Evans is a great teacher.

A I'm not sure I get it.

B I think so too.

C Sorry, but that's right.

Tip: Think carefully about the grammar *and* the meaning before choosing your answer.

1 Mr Evans is a great teacher.
  A I'm not sure I get it.
  (B) I think so too.
  C Sorry, but that's right.
2 Would you like to go to the park?
  A Yes, I want it.
  B I don't go.
  C I'd love to.
3 This weather is lovely.
  A I agree with you.
  B Oh right.
  C Now I get it.
4 When are you going to see Mark?
  A Two days ago.
  B He's in the classroom.
  C At 6.30.
5 Let's play a computer game.
  A Do you know what I mean?
  B I see.
  C That's a good idea!
6 How do I get to the cinema?
  A You can't miss it.
  B It's opposite the supermarket, at the end of the road.
  C There is a cinema.

4 **Complete the telephone conversation between two friends. Match gaps 1–6 with sentences A–H.**

Tip: Remember there are two extra sentences you do not need.

A: Hi, Matt! You aren't on holiday!
B: 1 *E*
A: You're right. But I didn't see you on the train this morning.
B: 2 ___
A: Really? He usually goes to work early.
B: 3 ___
A: That's good. Were the roads busy?
B: 4 ___
A: Wow! That was fast. Are you getting a lift home this afternoon?
B: 5 ___
A: That's good. You can help me with my French homework.
B: 6 ___
A: Very! For me! It's an exercise about verbs. I don't understand it.

A No, it was very quiet. There weren't many cars. I was at school in half an hour.
B Ah, OK. No, my dad drove me to school today.
C Have a good time!
D No worries. Is it hard?
E No, that's next week! I told you.
F No, I'm getting the train as usual.
G I love French. See you at the station.
H Yes, but today he started later. I saved some money!

5 **Read Petra's blog post about her bad week. Mark the sentences A (right), B (wrong) or C (doesn't say).**

Tip: Sometimes you need to read more than just one sentence to get the right answer.

Hi, everyone! I'm online again – wonderful! Now I can tell you about my terrible week. You know my dad works for a holiday company. He loves it and we don't have to pay much for our holidays – great! Well, last month he got a better job, with more money in the same company. But there was a problem. The job was in London and we lived in Manchester! So, last week we moved. Now we're in London, in a lovely house opposite a park. It's nice because we're near the centre and the shops are fantastic!

But last week was hard. I started a new school and it's OK but I really loved my old school. I had a lot of good friends and brilliant teachers. I'm sure I'm going to make new friends soon but it's difficult when you don't know people.

Another thing – in Manchester I walked to school every day but now my school is five kilometres away and I have to get public transport. The bus is always busy and I can't sit down. Also last week we didn't have wi-fi in the house! Terrible! I couldn't chat online, check emails or post on my blog. I had to read books, watch TV or do my homework. Boring!

1 Petra's dad is on holiday.
A Right (B) Wrong C Doesn't say

2 Petra's family get cheap holidays.
A Right B Wrong C Doesn't say

3 Her dad moved to a different company last month.
A Right B Wrong C Doesn't say

4 Now he works in London.
A Right B Wrong C Doesn't say

5 Petra can see a park from her room.
A Right B Wrong C Doesn't say

6 The teachers at her new school are very good.
A Right B Wrong C Doesn't say

7 She prefers walking to school to getting the bus.
A Right B Wrong C Doesn't say

8 Last week she enjoyed reading books and watching TV.
A Right B Wrong C Doesn't say

6 **Read the article about a town in England. Choose the best word (A, B or C) for each gap.**

Tip: Try to think of a word that fits the gap before you read the options. Sometimes you will know the answer quickly.

Winchester

If you are in the south of England, you [1]___ visit Winchester. This is [2]___ beautiful, quiet town with [3]___ old buildings. People who like history can visit old city walls, museums and a wonderful cathedral – perhaps the [4]___ in Europe!

Today London is the [5]___ important town in the UK but many centuries [6]___ it was Winchester. Kings and Queens of England lived [7]___ . Now, of course, they live in Buckingham Palace [8]___ London. Today Winchester is popular for tourists and for students! It has a very old and very famous school: Winchester College.

	A	B	C
1	have	need	(C) must
2	the	some	a
3	much	lots	many
4	longer	longest	long
5	most	more	very
6	early	last	ago
7	it	there	in
8	at	in	on

7 Read the descriptions of some words about technology. What is the word for each one? The first letter is already there.

Tip: Think what part of speech you need. The words are usually nouns but they can also be verbs or adjectives.

1 You need this for your phone to keep it working. **c**_harger_
2 When you wash your hair, you use this. **h**_ _ _ _ _ _ _
3 This is music on your phone that tells you someone is calling. **r**_ _ _ _ _ _ _
4 We need this for our TVs, radios, cookers, etc. **e**_ _ _ _ _ _ _ _ _ _
5 We can carry this in our pockets and use it to make phone calls and go online. **s**_ _ _ _ _ _ _ _ _
6 This is a place you visit on your computer to find information. **w**_ _ _ _ _ _

8 Complete the email. Write ONE word for each gap.

Tip: Think about the meaning of the whole sentence with the gap, not just a few words. Your word must fit both the grammar and the meaning.

To: tom@fastmessage.com

Hi Tom,

I saw [1]_your_ advert in the school magazine and I need some help! I've [2]________ a problem with my computer. The computer is very old. I've saved some money, but I haven't got [3]________ to buy a new one. [4]________ I go online, it's very slow. Sometimes [5]________ are messages, but I don't understand [6]________ . [7]________ night it didn't start and I couldn't send emails or work on it. Today [8]________ is working again.

[9]________ you help me? [10]________ number is 09784563124. I [11]________ staying home this evening so you can call me then.

Best wishes,
Lydia Green

9 Read the advert and the email. Complete Beth's notes.

Tip: Read both the advert and the email carefully before you start the task.

Charity Run!
Sunday morning in Green Park
10.00 until??
Run for charity!
Run longer = more money!
See you there!

From: Jack;
To: Beth;

Ben and I are going to run in this. I think it's going to be fun. Do you want to come? It's for a children's charity, Kidz. Call me on 0789689563421 if you want to do this. We can meet at the car park at 9.45. Don't forget to bring some water. It's going to be a hot day!

Beth's notes

Charity run in: [1]Green Park
Day: [2]
Which charity? [3]
Time to meet: [4]
Jack's number: [5]
Take: [6]

10 Read the email from your friend Jed.

Tip: Remember to count the words in your email. Don't go over or below the limit.

From: Jed;
To:

It's Sally's birthday on Saturday and I want to buy her a CD. What music does she like? Why don't we buy her a cake? Or can you bake one?

Write an email to Jed and answer the questions. Write 25–35 words.

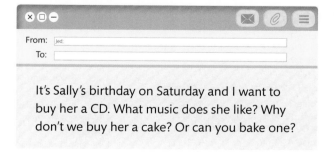

Unit 1

Exercise 1
1 Irish 2 American 3 Italy
4 Polish 5 France 6 Germany

Exercise 2
1 aunt 2 daughter 3 wife
4 grandmother 5 son 6 father

Exercise 3
1 slim 2 hat 3 sunglasses
4 dress 5 brave 6 grey

Exercise 4
1 Can you speak German?
2 My sister can't walk ten kilometres.
3 We can learn Spanish at my school.
4 Can your brother play football? Yes, he can.
5 Where can we buy new trainers?
6 Our teacher can't find our homework.
7 Can you do this exercise? No, I can't.
8 They can't help us.

Exercise 5
1 Gina hasn't got a nice dress for the party.
Has Gina got a nice dress for the party?
2 You haven't got two brothers.
Have you got two brothers?
3 Pete and Tom haven't got a new car.
Have Pete and Tom got a new car?
4 We haven't got an English test today.
Have we got an English test today?
5 I haven't got a problem with my computer.
Have I got a problem with my computer?
6 Grant hasn't got a black jacket.
Has Grant got a black jacket?
7 Ian's sister hasn't got long hair.
Has Ian's sister got long hair?

Exercise 6
1 e 2 a 3 c 4 d 5 b

Exercise 7
1 going 2 fine/good 3 How 4 I'm 5 This
6 meet 7 name's 8 Nice/Pleased 9 See

Unit 2

Exercise 1
1 butter 2 eggs 3 ketchup 4 grapes 5 milk
6 ice cream 7 baked beans 8 oil

Exercise 2
1 h 2 e 3 f 4 a 5 d 6 g 7 b 8 c

Exercise 3
1 c 2 a 3 c 4 b 5 a 6 c 7 a 8 b
9 c 10 b

Exercise 4
1 There's 2 Are 3 a 4 some, some
5 Is 6 aren't

Exercise 5
1 much 2 any 3 many 4 any 5 a 6 aren't
7 some, any 8 too 9 enough 10 lot

Exercise 6
1 f 2 d 3 e 4 a 5 b 6 c

Unit 3

Exercise 1
1 get 2 has, goes 3 watch 4 go 5 up
6 check 7 do 8 to 9 with

Exercise 2
1 budgies 2 hamster 3 pony 4 tortoise

Exercise 3
1 excited 2 tired 3 unhappy 4 sad
5 relaxed 6 worried 7 bored

Exercise 4
1 has 2 don't like 3 exercise
4 doesn't relax, does 5 speak 6 don't go

Exercise 5
1 Do you often chat with your friends online?
2 How much homework does your teacher give you?
3 When does your dad go to work?
4 Where do you have lunch at school?
5 What languages does your brother speak?
6 How does your mum get to work?

Exercise 6
1 kind 2 favourite 3 of 4 mind
5 stand 6 prefer 7 quite, hate

Unit 4

Exercise 1
1 whiteboard 2 calculator 3 eraser
4 pencil case 5 exercise book 6 text book
7 poster 8 ruler

Exercise 2
1 Geography 2 Art 3 Maths 4 History
5 IT 6 Biology 7 English 8 PE

Exercise 3
1 do 2 go 3 have 4 revise 5 start

Exercise 4
1 am laughing 2 are you talking 3 isn't working
4 Are Harry and Pete going 5 Is Tom wearing
6 is having

Exercise 5
1 have, are looking 2 don't need, isn't raining
3 work, am working 4 paints, is painting
5 am not doing, am talking

Exercise 6
1 in, on 2 behind 3 next to, next to
4 in front of 5 under 6 between

Exercise 7
1 Can, sorry 2 borrow, No 3 course 4 me, just

Unit 5

Exercise 1
1 piano 2 accordion 3 flute 4 violin
5 guitar 6 keyboards 7 saxophone 8 trumpet

Exercise 2
1 fantastic 2 brilliant 3 great 4 terrible
5 boring 6 cool 7 alright

Exercise 3
1 band 2 audience 3 stage
4 musician 5 rock

Exercise 4
1 better 2 cheaper 3 more excited
4 more difficult 5 worse 6 happier

Exercise 5
1 b 2 b 3 a 4 b 5 a 6 b

Exercise 6
1 What 2 Have 3 Can 4 Why 5 That's
6 Let's 7 Why 8 What/How

Unit 6

Exercise 1
1 Tennis 2 Archery 3 Ice hockey 4 Basketball

Exercise 2
1 Cup 2 score 3 points 4 team 5 pitch
6 cyclist, medals

Exercise 3
1 courts 2 go 3 running
4 lost 5 do 6 field

Exercise 4
1 was 2 weren't 3 Were
4 was 5 Was, were 6 wasn't, was

Exercise 5
1 saw 2 watched, shouted, scored 3 went
4 ran, won 5 played 6 ended, waited

Exercise 6
1 He arrived half an hour ago.
2 They built this house ten years ago.
3 We started the test fifteen minutes ago.
4 Sue and Ed/Ed and Sue went on holiday two months ago.
5 We got a new teacher three weeks ago.

Exercise 7
1 What, go 2 free, play 3 hang 4 into, fan 5 do, keen

Unit 7

Exercise 1
1 hairdryer 2 kettle 3 webcam 4 electric toothbrush
5 earphones 6 MP3 player 7 smartphone

Exercise 2
1 theory 2 ringtone 3 track 4 washing machine
5 console 6 invention 7 networking 8 engine

Exercise 3
1 wrote 2 understood 3 became
4 could 5 thought 6 sold

Exercise 4
1 I didn't do my English homework but I did my Maths homework.
2 I ate the meat but I didn't eat the vegetables.
3 Ella went to Mike's party but she didn't go to Henry's party.
4 We had Biology today but we didn't have History.
5 My parents didn't learn French at school but they learned English.

Exercise 5
1 When did you get home from London?
2 Where did you stay in London?
3 Who did you meet in Trafalgar Square?
4 What did you have for dinner?
5 How did you travel to London and back?

Exercise 6
1 so 2 maybe/perhaps 3 disagree
4 right 5 sure 6 agree

Unit 8

Exercise 1
1 c 2 b 3 a 4 d 5 f 6 e

Exercise 2
1 fluently 2 made 3 posted
4 native 5 capital 6 sent

Exercise 3
1 about 2 for 3 at 4 about 5 for 6 to

Exercise 4
1 don't have to 2 has to 3 mustn't
4 don't have to 5 have to 6 have to 7 mustn't

Exercise 5
1 a, The 2 a, an, The, the 3 A, a, the 4 a, the 5 a, the

Exercise 6
1 understand 2 right, it 3 sure
4 Now 5 see 6 mean

Unit 9

Exercise 1
1 car park 2 underground 3 motorbike
4 bus stop 5 bike lane 6 coach

Exercise 2
1 by 2 for 3 into 4 off 5 on

Exercise 3
1 b 2 d 3 c 4 e 5 a

Exercise 4
1 rainy 2 snowy 3 foggy 4 sunny 5 windy

Exercise 5
1 He's meeting Jack at the train station at 8.30.
2 He's having a History test on Friday morning.
3 He's swimming in a competition on Saturday afternoon.
4 He's going to art club at 4.15 today.
5 He's catching the 9.15 train to London tomorrow morning.
6 He's having a barbecue on Sunday afternoon at 2.30.

Exercise 6
1 am going to go 2 is going to call 3 is going to visit
4 am going to work 5 are going to buy
6 is going to correct

Exercise 7
1 Where 2 end 3 turn 4 on 5 there
6 past 7 take 8 next 9 for 10 get
11 at 12 straight 13 miss